CONSUMPTION

Consumption aims to provide a critical overview of major sociological approaches to the process of consumption in modern and post-modern societies. It develops a distinctive approach to the role of consumption as a socio-cultural process and to the ideology of consumerism. The role of consumption in early modern western society is examined, before an analysis of the emergence of consumption in the early twentieth century is given. This historical analysis provides the launching pad for an analysis of consumption between the 1950s and the present day. The author examines the contribution of leading writers in the field, including Veblen, Simmel, Marx, Gramsci, Weber, Bourdieu, Lacan and Baudrillard.

The book will appeal to students of sociology, cultural studies and communication studies.

Robert Bocock is Senior Lecturer in Sociology at the Open University.

KEY IDEAS
Series Editor: Peter Hamilton
The Open University

KEY IDEAS
Series Editor: PETER HAMILTON
The Open University, Milton Keynes

Designed to complement the successful *Key Sociologists*, this series covers the
main concepts, issues, debates, and controversies in sociology and the social
sciences. The series aims to provide authoritative essays on central topics of
social science, such as community, power, work, sexuality, inequality, benefits
and ideology, class, family, etc. Books adopt a strong individual 'line' constituting
original essays rather than literary surveys, and form lively and original
treatments of their subject matter. The books will be useful to students and
teachers of sociology, political science, economics, psychology, philosophy, and
geography.

THE SYMBOLIC CONSTRUCTION OF COMMUNITY
ANTHONY P. COHEN, Department of Social Anthropology, University of
Manchester
SOCIETY
DAVID FRISBY and DEREK SAYER, Department of Sociology, University
of Glasgow
SEXUALITY
JEFFREY WEEKS, Social Work Studies Department, University of
Southampton
WORKING
GRAEME SALAMAN, Faculty of Social Sciences, The Open University,
Milton Keynes
BELIEFS AND IDEOLOGY
KENNETH THOMPSON, Faculty of Social Sciences, The Open University,
Milton Keynes
EQUALITY
BRYAN TURNER, School of Social Sciences, The Flinders University of South
Australia
HEGEMONY
ROBERT BOCOCK, Faculty of Social Sciences, The Open University, Milton
Keynes
RACISM
ROBERT MILES, Department of Sociology, University of Glasgow
POSTMODERNITY
BARRY SMART, Department of Sociology, University of Auckland
CLASS
STEPHEN EDGELL, Department of Sociology, University of Salford
CULTURE
CHRIS JENKS, Department of Sociology, University of London

CONSUMPTION

ROBERT BOCOCK

London and New York

First published 1993
by Routledge
11 New Fetter Lane, London EC4P 4EE

Simultaneously published in the USA and Canada
by Routledge
29 West 35th Street, New York, NY 10001

Reprinted in 1995, 1997, 2000

Routledge is an imprint of the Taylor & Francis Group

Typeset in Times by Intype, London
Printed and bound in Great Britain by
Clays Ltd, St Ives plc

British Library Cataloguing in Publication Data
A catalogue record for this book is available
from the British Library

Library of Congress Cataloguing in Publication Data
A catalogue record for this book is available from
the Library of Congress

ISBN 0-415-06962-9

Biographical note

Dr Robert Bocock is Senior Lecturer in Sociology at the Open University, Walton Hall, Milton Keynes, England. He also lectures in sociology at the Richmond Fellowship College in London on courses for clergy, members of religious orders and lay people training to become counsellors.

Robert Bocock is author of *Ritual in Industrial Society* (1974); *Freud and Modern Society* (1976); *Sigmund Freud* (1983); and *Hegemony* (1986). He is also a contributor to, and editor, with K. Thompson, of *Religion and Ideology* (1985); and *Social and Cultural Forms of Modernity* (1992).

He has done research on ritual action in England and in Tanzania, funded by what is now the ESRC. He has also researched therapeutic approaches to deviance in Britain, the United States and Canada, the latter funded by the Nuffield Foundation.

Contents

Preface

Consumption has emerged from my earlier work on ritual, psychoanalytic sociology, and the sociology of religion and belief systems. There is a set of related theoretical issues which underlie these more substantive concerns. One of these is the usefulness or otherwise of critical theory for the analysis of modern societies. The critical theorists became over-shadowed by the development of structuralism, especially in the 1970s and 1980s. My concern has been to work out how far these schools of social theory are compatible or not.

Both approaches, of critical theory and structuralism, have used concepts and theoretical ideas derived from both Marx and Freud. The difference between those who have written within what might be called a broadly critical theoretical paradigm, and those who have used a structuralist paradigm, lies in their respective approaches to Hegel. The critical theorists could be described as using Hegelian ideas, such as the claim that Reason was, or could be, operating in world history. Critical theory was, therefore, historicist in that it sought to discover a meaning in historical events. The structuralists were negative about these concerns derived from Hegel, and sought to develop an anti-humanist, non-historicist, 'scientific', approach to the analysis of culture and society.

Be that as it may, I have found that the theoretical anti-humanism of structuralism was unsatisfactory. The perennial problem of the social sciences has concerned the sense in which they could ever be said to be 'sciences' in any meaningful way at all. Structuralism has not been able to resolve this problem, as it had appeared to be able to do at one stage.

This book reflects my concern with these epistemological and wider philosophical issues. However, it always seems a good idea to become involved with trying to make sense of some concrete issue in sociology, rather than trying to resolve the philosophical issues at a purely abstract level. By so doing, some of the issues do seem to resolve themselves into being less serious than they might otherwise appear. I have found, for instance, that the issue about the usefulness of psychoanalytic ideas in looking at consumption helps to lessen the gulf between the critical theorist, Herbert Marcuse, and the supposedly structuralist psychoanalyst, Jacques Lacan. There is less of a gulf between them than calling one of them an Hegelian critical theorist, and the other a structuralist might suggest (see Chapter 4). But this kind of opposition lay behind the turn to structuralism, away from critical theory, which followed the 1968 events in Paris.

Consumption will no doubt cease to be the fascinating topic it was during the 1980s – fascinating that is to sociologists, not just to customers. Such are the vagaries of modern, or post-modern, capitalism that no sooner had consumption 'taken off' in the 1980s than a deep recession developed in Britain and in the United States in the early 1990s. However, the issues raised in this book are not ones which will go away just because there are periods of deep economic recession from time to time. Consumption now affects the ways in which people build up, and maintain, a sense of who they are, of who they wish to be. It has become entwined with the processes surrounding the development of a sense of identity. As such it will remain an important social, psychological and cultural process, as well as an economic one.

Acknowledgements

Working on courses at the Open University has provided one of the main contexts within which my interest in the concept of, and theories about, consumption developed. In particular, the members of the course teams of the new social science foundation course for the 1990s, 'Society and Social Science', and of the second level course, 'Understanding Modern Societies', have provided much stimulus and criticism. Stuart Hall, Kenneth Thompson, Doreen Massey, James Anderson, David Held, Kay Pole, Andrew Northedge, Marilyn Ricci, David Coates, Margaret Wetherell, Vivienne Brown and Elaine Storkey were among those who provided valuable criticism and support in the development of my interests in consumption.

Staff and students at the Richmond Fellowship College, London, have also provided a valuable stimulus and a context in which some ideas about consumption could be discussed. I have given lectures and seminars in sociology and social psychology on two courses at this college during the time this book was being thought about and written. The college provides courses in applied social science for pastoral care workers, clergy and members of religious orders, people who are on the whole removed from many of the pressures to consume which operate on the rest of us. Their perspective on consumption has affected the conclusion to this book. In particular John Wickens, Herman Bommer, Sky Siney and Michael Kelly have discussed their ideas about consumption from time to time in a helpful way.

Other people whose help, support and criticism have provided a stimulus for this book have been the editor of the series, Peter Hamilton, and the Senior Editor in Sociology at Routledge, Chris Rojek. Also Jean Bocock, June Huntington, Michael Bowman, Alfonso Moreno and Olive Wilson have provided much help and support during the writing process.

None of these is responsible for any errors or misinterpretations which may be found in this book. But my thanks are due to them all for support during the process of production.

Introduction

Why did the activities associated with consumption in western societies become an exciting subject for study in sociology? It might be thought that consumption is more a matter of interest to economists, or to advertisers and market researchers, rather than to sociologists, social psychologists or social theorists. A part of the answer to the question goes back to events in the 1960s, events which affected developments in social theory.

In the 1960s there was what the German critical theorist Jurgen Habermas termed 'a legitimation crisis' in the advanced western societies (Habermas, 1976). This took the form, in part, of a protest movement among students, and among other young people in various forms of work from industrial production to commercial work. The protest had been against education and training becoming more oriented towards the needs of the industrial and commercial organisations of advanced capitalism, to the neglect of wider concerns, such as the issue of poverty, and malnutrition, of philosophy and aesthetics. There had also been a protest against the Vietnam War – a war which seemed to epitomise the misuse of scientific talents and technological resources by the United States, in particular, in the eyes of many

young people. To such groups, the political decision-making processes in the West appeared to be at fault, producing a crisis of
legitimation in the area of the political system.

This period did not, however, lead to major changes in the
political system, nor in the economic system of western capitalism. Rather it could be said that by the end of the 1980s capitalism had become legitimated among the majority of the popu-
lations living in the western societies, and among some living
elsewhere. The changes in Eastern Europe and the Soviet Union,
during the late 1980s, for instance, partly derived from the attrac-
tions of capitalism in the eyes of many living in these former
communist societies. Capitalism appeared attractive and legitimated in much of the West, and in the Eastern Bloc, because it
provided, or seemed to provide, consumer goods, which people
wanted.

The consumption of goods and services became possible for
more and more groups in western societies, in Japan and in other
parts of South East Asia, during the last half of the twentieth
century. Consumption as a set of social, cultural and economic
practices, together with the associated ideology of consumerism,
has served to legitimate capitalism in the eyes of millions of
ordinary people, if not in the hearts and minds of those former
protesters of the 1960s.

Alongside these social, political and cultural events which have
brought consumption to the forefront of some sociologists' attention, there has been an important change within social theory
which also served to focus attention upon consumption. This was
the development of the approach known broadly as 'structuralism'. Structuralism had been developed, in its post-Second World
War form, by the French anthropologist Claude Lévi-Strauss. He
had developed it for the analysis of societies without written
languages – that is for pre-literate societies. He had emphasised
the role that signs and symbols played in 'structures' of myth and
ritual in such societies. Those who were concerned with the
analysis of modern societies, which contained *written* language,
were struck by the importance of signs and symbols in these
cultures too. This did not mean that the signs and symbols in the
mass media of these societies had necessarily replaced the written
word completely, but structuralism served to highlight the importance of such signs and symbols in industrial societies too. The
role of signs and symbols was very marked in one of the central
processes in such modern societies, that of consumption, and in

the associated ideology of consumerism, as seen particularly in the various forms of advertisements for consumer goods.

Consumption, in late twentieth-century western forms of capitalism, may be seen, therefore, as a social and cultural process involving cultural signs and symbols, not simply as an economic, utilitarian process. It is the social and cultural aspects of the process which are to be the main focus here. This approach is not intended, however, to convey the impression that economic factors do not matter. Both in the advanced societies of capitalism, and in those social formations which remain predominantly rural and agriculturally based, there are many groups whose economic situation largely determines their patterns of consumption, rather than the social and cultural factors to be discussed here. Nevertheless, once people have been influenced by what might be called the social and cultural practices associated with the ideology of modern consumerism, then even if they cannot afford to buy the goods portrayed in films, in the press and on television, they can and do *desire* them.

Consumption is seen here, therefore, as being based increasingly upon desires, not simply upon need (Baudrillard, 1988: 10–56). This does not mean that this approach is to be understood as a replacement for a more materialistic, economic one, for the latter approach is still relevant in some parts of the world, and among the poorest groups in western capitalism, as indicated above. In the social formations of western capitalism, however, consumption has become linked with desires, through the use of signs and symbols in selling products to the majority of consumers. These desires to become a certain type of person through consuming objects such as clothes, or styles of furniture, do not disappear in periods of economic recession. They may continue to affect people who remain employed, and even some among the unemployed. They may lie dormant for a while, waiting to be reactivated when the green light is given again and disposable incomes rise.

Consumption became an important concept in sociology, and in social theory more generally, during the 1980s. The focus upon consumption was part of a wider debate about post-modernity – that is about whether or not western capitalism had undergone a significant change, so deep-rooted that it required a new theoretical orientation which was to be signalled by the term 'postmodern'. If 'modern' implied an industrial, urban, capitalist society, in which socio-economic class was still the determining feature of people's lives, of their sense of who they were, their identity, 'post-modern' implied a post-industrial, suburban, even post-capitalist social formation in which old, stable points for establishing people's sense of identity had been displaced. Identities in post-modern conditions become more flexible and float around in a state of potential, if not actual, change (Bauman, 1992).

Consumption has been seen as epitomising this move into post-modernity, for it implies a move away from productive work roles being central to people's lives, to their sense of identity, of who they are. In place of work roles, it is roles in various kinds of family formations, in sexual partnerships of various kinds, in leisure-time pursuits, in consumption in general, which have come to be seen as being more and more significant to people. These concerns have become reflected in sociology and social theory as a debate about whether or not western societies are moving towards becoming 'post-modern' (Featherstone, 1991).

The interest in consumption, in the context of this debate about whether capitalism has changed so fundamentally that it can be described as 'post-modern', has picked up some themes which were first introduced into sociology in the late nineteenth and early twentieth centuries. One example was the role of consumption among the North East American industrial and commercial bourgeoisie, who had won in the Civil War (1861–65) against the older land-owning and slave-owning class based in the south. These two groups had been analysed by Veblen, an American sociologist, at the turn of the last century. Veblen's analysis will be discussed in Chapter 1.

Was this bourgeois leisure class the first to live in modern capitalism in this way, as a group dedicated to consumption? Did it set a precedent for what developed later in the United States, and then in Western Europe? It was one of the first, if not the first, class, or class fraction (that is a component part of a larger class like the American bourgeoisie in this case), within modern capitalism to live for consumption, not to live for work. Other classes had lived as a leisured class in other types of social formation, such as the aristocracies in European feudalism, but a specifically bourgeois class, or part thereof, within modern capitalism, had not done so on the same scale as the group which Veblen analysed. Later in the twentieth century, more and more North Americans in the working and middle classes became consumers, but not, of course, a leisured class.

In Britain, and other European societies, it was not until the 1950s that consumption became more widespread among the general population, although the forms of mass consumption which developed in this period were not based upon a leisured class – for people had to do paid work to obtain money to buy consumer goods. The decade of the 1950s was important in the development of consumption in modern capitalism. The 1980s was not the first decade of consumption, therefore. Whether or not consumption in the 1950s and early 1960s was different from that in the 1980s will have to be explored in the light of the various factors which shaped the patterns of consumption in the two periods. Unless it can be established that the latter is significantly different from the former period, consumption cannot be used as the way to demarcate post-modernity. The question to be asked is whether or not there can be shown to be theoretically significant differences between consumption in the two periods to such a degree that a conceptual distinction between them can be supported (see Smart, 1993: 64).

The concept of consumption has a variety of meanings, depending upon the major theoretical framework of which it is a component part. The concept of consumption has been used by some sociologists, for instance, in a way which is distinct from its role in economic theories, whether these were monetarist, Keynesian or Marxist theoretical frameworks. As sociologists developed their analyses of *social* action, as distinct from political or economic actions, so they focused on consumption as a social activity, rather than as a primarily economic activity, linked to demand and supply, to production, to money supply or to interest rates. In Max Weber's sociological analysis, for instance, which has played a major part in the subsequent development of sociology as a distinctive theoretical discourse, the concept of *social status* was developed. This entailed that, for a Weberian analysis of modern capitalism, in addition to *economic classes*, defined in terms of either ownership of significant amounts of capital in the form of productive industry, or in the form of commercial property, or in the more abstract form of financial capital such as shares, bonds, bank deposits or currency (a definition of economic class which is congruent with that of Marx), there are other groups who may act in ways which affect historical developments. These were social status groups and political parties (Giddens, 1971).

A social status group is defined as a group which acts in a

variety of ways, including intra-group marriage, social mechanisms which include some and exclude others, such as notions of ritual pollution, in order to preserve their distinctive social group. These are not only relatively trivial matters, such as table manners, or ways of speaking, but may include the use of armed force to preserve a status group's way of life (see also Elias, 1978). A status group, by definition, has a distinctive pattern of living, of eating, drinking, dressing, entertaining, in short of consuming. Such patterns help to define the members of a status group, to preserve its status-honour, its social and cultural esteem, in its own eyes, and in the eyes of others in the social formation who share the same cultural values. For example, members of a Royal Family are seen at the apex of one system of status-honour by those who are not Royals themselves, but who share Royalist cultural values. Those groups who do not share such Royalist values, but are more oriented to achievement in business, entertainment or sports, will see different types of person as being at the top of the social status hierarchy. Whichever kind of group, or groups, are given high social status, and the associated publicity in the mass media, the patterns of consumption of such groups are reported upon and emulated by some in the relevant audiences.

The overall theoretical perspective for this analysis of consumption in capitalism, however, is one which could be best described as Gramscian. This term connotes here a theoretical perspective based upon the analysis of the mode of production of capitalism, but an approach which eschews economism – that is the claim that the economic production base determines what happens in the political, cultural, religious, or consumption, areas of a society's life (Bocock, 1986). The economic mode of production sets the basic parameters within which other activities, including consumption, occur, but does not determine, or necessarily affect in very direct ways, such activities. Furthermore, this position is compatible with much of what Marx analysed as being characteristic features of capitalism as a mode of production – the use of *profit* as the measure of all things, not human needs and requirements. Food, for example, goes to those who can buy it at a price which produces a profit for the wholesaler, the retailer and the producer, the farmer. Adequate food does not go to those who may need it most – the hungry or starving people in Africa, Asia or South America, or to the poor in the western capitalist societies.

This much would be agreed by Weber too, as both Gramsci and Giddens in their different ways have argued (Giddens, 1971: 185–224). Weber need not be seen as replacing a Marxist analysis of modern capitalism, but as adding to it. Both Weberian and Gramscian perspectives give a considerable degree of relative autonomy to culture, to symbols as some anthropologists analyse such phenomena. A Gramscian perspective can also find an important place for psychoanalysis in understanding the influence and power of some cultural symbol systems as we shall see in Chapter 4, something lacking in most Weberian approaches.

The approach to consumption which is developed in this book is an *extension*, not a direct application, of the non-economistic, more broadly philosophical approach of Gramsci, for he did not develop his ideas in the context of the consumer-oriented capitalism of the second half of the twentieth century, but in that of Italian fascism in the 1920s and 1930s. The central concept that Gramsci developed – hegemony – that is intellectual, moral and political, but *not* military, leadership in a social formation – remains useful, however, in understanding the social, cultural, political and economic changes and developments of the post–1950 period, up to the 1990s, in western capitalism. Consumption as a social-economic activity, and the associated ideological practices of consumerism, can be seen as having aimed to move into a hegemonic position in these social formations in that period. However, consumption, and the ideology of consumerism, could never be said to be hegemonic in a Gramsciam sense, because that would entail the view that consumerism, and the associated practices of consumption, could form a viable moral philosophical whole way of living among all human beings on the earth. If it were the case that, in contradistinction to various positivisms and to the relativism implicit in much post-modernism, it is possible to articulate a rationally grounded philosophy which locates consumption as a *means* to the fulfilment of human living, but not as the sole *goal* of social, cultural and economic life, as Gramscians would claim, consumption and consumerism cannot be seen as capable of being truly hegemonic. For this to be possible, the social, cultural and economic practices associated with consumption would have to be grounded philosophically in a world-view such as that of free-market liberalism, based on concepts such as the free market, and the individual, there being no such entity as 'society' in such a viewpoint, only individuals competing with one another in markets to sell goods, services,

or their manual, or mental, labouring abilities. If such a philosophical world-view is rejected, some other must take its place,
or there is a relapse into relativism.

It can be seen from what has just been said that, in the perspective which lies behind this book, the human sciences are linked
logically, and inescapably, with philosophy, including epistem-
ology, moral and political philosophy, philosophy of history and
ontology (that is what there ultimately is in the universe – matter,
energy or some life-force pushing towards higher and higher
forms of consciousness). The human sciences cannot be detached
from this philosophical underpinning as various forms of positiv-
sm have sought to do.

Any conception of how we can find and gain knowledge about
the social, political, economic, cultural and psychological aspects
of life is, logically, grounded in some philosophical conception
or other. Social scientists cannot avoid this, especially not by
declaring an approach to be 'scientific' for this term begs all the
questions: What counts as knowledge? How can knowledge about
societies be generated? Can people affect what goes on in world
history? What goals should be pursued in political economy and
in culture? (See MacIntyre, 1988.) These questions cannot be
answered here. Some answers to them do, however, underpin
the approach which is taken in that the broad perspective underlying the analysis of consumption is based upon the view that all
social scientific analysis of this type involves values because language is always a carrier of a moral philosophy, as will become
clearer in the following chapters.

The first chapter of this book will discuss the main features of
the ways in which sociologists have studied consumption and how
they have seen its role in the twentieth century. Specific attention
will be given to consumption patterns in Britain since the end of
the Second World War. This will provide a basic overview of the
main empirical features of modern consumption in Britain, but
with some mention of other western social formations. On this
basis, some decision may be made about similarities and differences between consumption in the 1950s and 1960s and that in
the 1980s.

Chapter 2 goes on to examine the main theoretical concepts
which are relevant to the analysis of modern consumption. These
include the concepts of commodities, cultural values and alienation.

The work of social scientists who were influenced by the work of structuralists on language and symbols has been important for the analysis of consumption. The work of Lévi-Strauss has been of particular importance for it formed a base from which later work on modern consumption was produced (as in the writings of Bourdieu and Baudrillard, whose work is discussed in this context). These ideas about consumption will be outlined and discussed in Chapter 3.

Chapter 4 discusses ideas about identity and their relationship to the study of consumption. It attempts to assess the usefulness of a Lacanian approach in understanding modern, or post-modern, consumption, especially in relation to desires and changes in the social and cultural construction of identity.

In the Conclusion, the threads of the argument are pulled together. Some final reflections upon where modern consumerism may be heading, and its impact upon other social institutions such as religion, will be included, for when consumerism has been challenged in the West, this challenge has come not so much from politicians but from religious figures, as well as from environmentalists.

1
The emergence of modern consumerism

The social and cultural processes surrounding consumption in western capitalism during the twentieth century have been influenced by earlier cultural values, carried by various social status groups into the modern capitalist period. Among these carriers of cultural values, the early rational, peaceable, bourgeois capitalists of Britain and Holland, whose world-view was analysed by the German sociologist Max Weber (1864–1920) in *The Protestant Ethic and the Spirit of Capitalism*, have played a crucial role of world historical significance. Their migration, sometimes forced upon them, across the Atlantic, laid the basis of the modern United States of America – the social formation which has come to epitomise the modern consumer's dreamland, or heaven on earth. The analysis Weber provided of this group, the early rational, Calvinist capitalists of the seventeenth century, will be discussed briefly here, before looking at later changes to this cultural patterning underpinning rational capitalism in the eighteenth century.

The changes in patterns of consumption during late nineteenth- and early twentieth-century capitalism, up to the outbreak of the First World War in 1914, will be discussed in the light of the sociology of consumption from Veblen and of the newly emerging metropolitan life-style analysed by Simmel. The period of the two world wars, and the intervening economic recession and depression of the 1920s and 1930s, was one in which capitalism failed to deliver consumer goods to the working classes. Reflecting this bleak and violent economic and political period, sociologists concentrated on other issues, such as the appeal of fascism, rather than upon consumption.

The story of the social and cultural role of consumption in modern, western capitalism continued with the growth of what was often called at the time, that is in the 1950s and 1960s, 'the growth of mass consumption'. There were some interesting features of mass consumption which have been seen as distinctive of the period from the early 1950s up to the late 1960s. From the 1970s to the 1980s, some writers have argued that a new, even 'post-modern' pattern of consumption developed. The significance of this will be explored in the last part of this chapter.

EARLY PATTERNS OF CONSUMPTION

The early patterning of consumption within a distinctively capitalist economic structure began to emerge in England during the post Civil War period, that is in the second half of the seventeenth century. Puritanism, especially in its Calvinist form, exercised considerable influence upon the early bourgeoisie of agricultural and manufacturing capitalism. This was a system of production which employed a legally free wage-labour force (as distinct from slaves or serfs) and which pursued the peaceful, systematic, rational generation of profits through the sale of commodities produced for a free market. Early capitalist forms of production affected British agriculture, for example, earlier than in the rest of Europe, where peasant farming continued. Commercial agriculture developed a 'free market' in farm land, in agricultural labour and in the sale of the foods, or other goods, produced on the new-style farms. Some of these new-style commercially oriented farmers were puritans; they were typically neither Roman, nor Anglican, Catholics (Weber, 1970). Puritanism also affected some of the early manufacturing capitalist families in a way which aided the growth of their businesses because they re-invested the profits which they made, rather than spending them on a luxurious life-style, as aristocrats and royal families had done in other social formations.

The important cultural legacy of puritanism has been a potent element in English, Welsh and Scottish cultures as well as the exported varieties of these in North America and Australasia. Puritanism affected these nations as a set of deeply embedded values, shared by many members of the elite groups in these countries (Ireland remained distinctive, with forms of both Protestant and Catholic puritanism embedded in a different political and historical structure from that of Britain).

British puritanism involved ascetic values such as not spending too much money on clothes, especially on clothing for men or boys, or upon eating elaborate and expensive meals. Houses were to be well built, furnished comfortably, but should not seem to be too elaborate in design or too garish in colour. These cultural values were not determined by economic factors, even if they were affected by shortages both in periods of economic depression and during the Second World War. Other societies with less Protestant, puritanical cultural values, such as France, Italy and Spain, have had values which have encouraged spending on what the British have traditionally defined as extravagant items – such as fashionable clothing, jewellery, eating and drinking well at home and in restaurants. These differences go back to the Reformation of the sixteenth century and to the Cromwellian government of the seventeenth century. As Max Weber wrote of this period:

> asceticism descended like a frost on the life of 'Merrie old England'. And not only worldly merriment felt its effect. The Puritan's ferocious hatred of everything which smacked of superstition, of all survivals of magical or sacramental salvation, applied to the Christmas festivities and the May Pole and all spontaneous religious art. . . .
>
> The theatre was obnoxious to the Puritans, and with the strict exclusion of the erotic and of nudity from the realm of toleration a radical view of either literature or art could not exist. The conceptions of idle talk, . . . of vain ostentation, all designations of an irrational attitude without objective purpose, thus not ascetic, and especially not serving the glory of God, but of man, were always at hand to serve in deciding in favour of sober utility as against artistic tendencies. This was especially true in the case of decoration of the person, for instance clothing. That powerful tendency toward uniformity of

life, which to-day so immensely aids the capitalistic
interest in the standardisation of production, had its ideal
foundations in the repudiation of all idolatry of the flesh.
(Weber, 1971: 168–9)

These cultural values, Weber argued, aided the development of
British capitalism in the early eighteenth century in both agriculture and early industrial developments. Puritanical values were
modified after the Restoration of the monarchy in England in
1688 – the theatre was allowed again, and clothing became subject
to fashion among well-to-do men and women, for instance (see
Campbell, 1987: Chapter 2). Yet something of the puritan out-
look did persist, and can still be drawn upon from time to time
by those seeking to control the expression of sexuality in the
theatre and other media, including cinema and television. This
pattern of legal and social controls has persisted into the last
decades of the twentieth century in Britain (Weeks, 1977).

Britain has had a relative degree of consensus about the less
stringent of these puritanical cultural values; few politicians of
any political party, few church leaders, have thought it prudent
to oppose them strongly. There was a brief period in the late
1960s and early 1970s when legal controls were relaxed over
theatre, cinema and publishing, but Britain remains subject to
more controls being exercised over the media of all forms than
many of its European neighbours, such as France or the Nether-
lands (Weeks, 1985).

The high degree of consensus found among the British political
and legal elites may be explained in part by the fact that Britain's
cultural and political values and institutions have not been radically altered in the recent past. Indeed, the events of 1688, when
the monarchy's powers were limited by Parliament, have been
the main underpinnings for all subsequent changes in English
constitutional debates and changes.

Before looking at more recent developments, however, it is
instructive to look at the earlier development of consumption in
the eighteenth century. During the eighteenth century small-scale
enterprises manufactured consumer goods such as pottery, clothing, jewellery, buttons and pins (Porter, 1990). The consumers
of these kinds of product were living not only in London, but in
Manchester, Liverpool, Birmingham, Bristol and Leeds, for the
development of canals and roads opened up these regional cities
to the cultural influence of London in the period from 1700 to

1750. Advertising began in the middle of the eighteenth century in provincial newspapers and periodicals, so that women in Newcastle knew about the 'latest' style in Wedgwood in the late 1780s, for example, as a result of the development of a strong provincial press (Porter, 1990). Manufacturing took place on a small scale, in small workshops, or in the household, through the process known as 'putting-out' in which manufacturers organised production of goods in the home. As R. Porter put it:

> Up to 1760, no decisive breakthroughs had occurred in mechanisation, in work organisation, in the scale of the workplace, in sources of industrial power. . . . Industry remained largely labour-intensive and skill-intensive. Weaving, smithying, hat-making, the furniture and cutlery trades, metal-working and thousands more besides expanded by recruiting more hands.
>
> (Porter, 1990: 193–5)

The first sixty years of the eighteenth century saw the development of 'a consumer revolution' in the sense of an increased number of people aware of, and able to purchase, an increasing variety of goods for the household, and for body decoration. This growth of an increased market for such consumer goods among the urban middle classes, as well as the aristocracy and country gentlefolk, preceded the development of larger-scale industrial production processes such as cotton manufacturing in Lancashire in the last three decades of the eighteenth century. Porter argues that such a development of consumption did provide the foundations for the later development of large-scale industrial production processes which began in the late eighteenth century and created the basis for nineteenth-century industrial capitalism in Britain (Porter, 1990). *Production processes* underwent major change and development between the 1770s and the 1870s. These new methods of factory manufacturing were introduced by a new class of capitalist entrepreneurs – people with new ideas creating the early capitalist mode of production. New classes developed – the industrial working classes who worked in heavy industry, in manufacturing and in distribution of goods; and the bourgeoisie, the owners of the new capitalist enterprises which were formed in the so-called 'industrial revolution' (Thompson, 1963).

The nineteenth-century changes were those which Karl Marx observed. He created social and economic theories about the structure of these changes and the processes by which the changes in production and consumption created a new mode of production – industrial capitalism. Some of his ideas will be discussed in Chapter 2. Before that, it is important to look at the ways in which sociologists have conceptualised the process of consumption, and its role in capitalist societies, from the late nineteenth century to the 1980s.

INDUSTRIAL CAPITALISM AND CONSUMPTION

Consumers, in the early modern period, may be defined as groups for whom patterns of consumption played a central role in their lives, providing them with ways of marking themselves off from other social status groups. This process also helped to provide them with a sense of social identity. Such groups of consumers began to emerge in the late nineteenth century in the United States and in Western Europe as industrial capitalism developed. One such group was the newly wealthy middle class in North America, who had made considerable amounts of money from trade and manufacturing. They were the focus of a study written by the American sociologist Thorstein Veblen (1857–1929). Veblen analysed the rich members of this group, seeing them as a new leisure class, who tried to ape the life-styles of the upper classes in Europe. Unlike the latter, they displayed their new-found wealth in what Veblen termed, in his memorable phrase, 'conspicuous consumption'.

Another group for whom consumption played a central role in daily living patterns were the inhabitants of the rapidly expanding German city of Berlin, at the turn of century. This group was observed, and their patterns of daily living analysed, by the German sociologist Georg Simmel (1858–1918). They were living in a new kind of environment – the early modern metropolis – which affected their way of life in significant ways, as we shall see.

The writings of these two sociologists became over-shadowed by the two world wars and the rise of fascism in Europe, as mentioned above. Sociologists became interested in their work in the 1980s, as the analysis of consumption was taken up again. Veblen and Simmel had begun to develop their sociology of new ways of life in western societies at the time when new department stores had opened for the first time, in the centres of big cities. These department stores offered to shoppers, all under one roof, a variety of goods from groceries, furniture, clothing, crockery, kitchen utensils, to new electrical equipment, as these latter products were developed and manufactured for a mass market.

Such city centre shops offered more choice than local ones were able to do, although groceries were obtainable in small corner shops, together with butchers, fishmongers, bakers and greengrocers in local shopping areas. The city centre department stores developed as trams, trolley buses and railways were built to take people into the centre of cities from the outlying suburban areas.

Cities such as Berlin, Paris, London, Glasgow, New York and Chicago expanded their transport networks and developed large city centre department stores from the 1890s up to the outbreak of the First World War in 1914. Paris had been redesigned and rebuilt by Haussmann in the 1860s to become a city of boulevards, suitable not only for soldiers to use to control riots among the poor, but also for *flâneurs* to stroll along, to display their clothes and to window shop. Simmel observed Berlin during the late nineteenth century – a city bulging with new migrants coming to live in it, especially from the East, including Poland. In his essay 'The metropolis and mental life' (1903) he argued that the modern city is 'not a spatial entity with sociological consequences, but a sociological entity that is formed spatially' (Frisby, 1984: 131). Cities grew around centres of government, or around particular industries, from steel-making to lace-making. The shops and leisure facilities of cities, such as theatres, music halls, sports stadia, and later on, the cinemas, all grew up to satisfy the social and psychological requirements of the inhabitants of the newly burgeoning towns and cities.

Furthermore, the daily lives of people who lived in a great metropolis, Simmel argued, were affected by the need to cultivate a 'blasé attitude' towards others:

> for it was only by screening out the complex stimuli that stemmed from the rush of modern life that we could tolerate its extremes. Our only outlet . . . is to cultivate a sham individualism through the pursuit of signs of status, fashion, or marks of individual eccentricity.
>
> (Harvey, 1989: 26)

Simmel went on to argue in his 1903 essay (1903: 318) that 'the deepest problems of modern life derive from the claim of the individual to preserve the autonomy of his existence in the face of overwhelming social forces'.

These problems were found especially in the modern metropolis. A recent sociologist, David Frisby, has commented on this idea, using some words from Simmel's 1903 essay, as follows:

> (The) individual must 'resist being levelled down and worn out by a social-technological mechanism' such as the metropolis. Extreme subjectivism is the response to the extreme objectification of culture that is found there. Hence the individual's struggle for self-assertion, when confronted with the pervasive indifference of much metropolitan social interaction, may take the form of stimulating a sense of distinctiveness, even in an excessive form of adopting 'the most tendentious eccentricities, the specifically metropolitan excesses of aloofness, caprice and fastidiousness, whose significance no longer lies in the content of such behaviour, but rather in its form of being different, of making oneself stand out and thus attracting attention'. In part, this arises out of 'the brevity and infrequency of meetings' which necessitates coming to the point as quickly as possible and making a striking impression in the briefest possible time.
>
> (Frisby, 1984: 131–2)

Modern patterns of consumption, therefore, in part result from living in the metropolis, the city and its suburbs, for this has given rise to a new kind of individual who is anxious, as Simmel expressed it, 'to preserve the autonomy and individuality of his existence in the face of overwhelming social forces'. Hence the need to avoid 'being levelled down and worn out by a social-technological mechanism' – the metropolis.

The processes involved in living in the city increase the awareness of style, of the need to consume within a repertory which is both distinctive to a specific social group and expressive of individual preferences. The metropolitan individual is no longer the older type which Max Weber had analysed in his work on Calvinism, who would not spend 'foolishly' on relatively trivial items of clothing or adornment, as mentioned above. Rather the person in the big city consumes in order to articulate a sense of identity, of who they wish to be taken to be. The body decoration and clothing, for example, which a particular individual uses as a means of marking themselves out from others, have to be interpreted and understood by others. So someone can only mark themselves as being different from others if they also share some common cultural signs with others.

This, in turn, produces a ceaseless striving for the *distinctive*, with the higher social status groups continually having to change their own patterns of consumption as the middle middle, lower middle classes, and most of the strata in the working class, copy some of their habits. For example, drinking champagne or malt whisky, once the preserve of the British aristocracy, has moved down the social status hierarchy in the last one hundred years, so that the upper social status groups either cease to drink these drinks, or consume more exclusive and expensive brand names.

This type of process had been observed by Veblen in the United States during the late nineteenth century. His ideas and observations were published in *The Theory of the Leisure Class*, first published in 1899, with a revised edition in 1912. Veblen was concerned with the American *nouveaux riches* of the late nineteenth century. These groups, he argued, tended to ape their own perceptions of European aristocratic ways of life – or they tried to do so, sometimes with strange consequences produced by misunderstandings. The lower middle classes and working classes, both black and white, were not yet caught up in these processes, for they were too poor. Veblen was interested in the new leisure class:

> The quasi-peaceable gentleman of leisure . . . consumes freely and of the best, in food, drink, narcotics, shelter, services, ornaments, apparel, weapons and accoutrements, amusements, amulets, and idols or divinities. . . .
>
> Closely related to the requirement that the gentleman must consume freely and of the right kind of goods, there is the requirement that he must know how to consume them in seemly manner. His life of leisure must be conducted in due form. Hence arise good manners . . . High-bred manners and ways of living are items of conformity to the norm of conspicuous leisure and conspicuous consumption.
>
> (Veblen, 1912 and 1953: 64)

Veblen also analysed the role of women in the American leisure class. For home furnishings, clothes, jewellery, eating and drinking expensive foods and alcoholic drinks, became central to the social lives of the leisured class, and these were activities which were typically organised by women. Wives and daughters were also used by men as a way of displaying their wealth, by showing that they could afford to buy expensive, fashionable things, or experiences, such as horse-riding or trips to Europe, for their women-folk. As Veblen wrote:

> it has in the course of economic development become the office of the woman to consume vicariously for the head of the household; and her apparel is contrived with this object in view. It has come about that obviously productive labour is in a peculiar degree derogatory to respectable women, and therefore special pains should be taken in the construction of women's dress to impress upon the beholder the fact (often indeed a fiction) that the wearer does not and cannot habitually engage in useful work. Propriety requires respectable women to abstain . . . from useful effort and to make more of a show of leisure than the men of the same social classes. It grates painfully on our nerves to contemplate the necessity of any well-bred woman's earning a livelihood by useful work. It is not 'women's sphere'. Her sphere is within the household, which she should beautify. . . .
>
> By virtue of its descent from a patriarchal past, our social system makes it the woman's function in an especial degree to put in evidence her household's ability to pay. According to the modern civilised scheme of life, the good name of the household to which she belongs should be the special care of the woman; and the system of honorific expenditure and conspicuous leisure by which this good name is chiefly sustained is therefore the woman's sphere.
>
> (Veblen, 1953: 126)

Veblen and Simmel both provided analyses of newly emerging life-styles at the turn of the century – a metropolitan, or *nouveau riche*, lifestyle in which the consumption of such things as clothes, personal adornments and expensive pleasurable pursuits was becoming central. Such patterns of living were spreading increasingly among other less affluent groups, as the twentieth century developed. The two world wars did not affect this process as much in the United States as they did in Europe, although Americans were affected by the economic depression of the 1930s. The development of a form of consumer-oriented capitalism was severely disrupted in Germany by political and military events until the 1950s.

Neither Veblen nor Simmel tried to develop social theories about the functioning of modern capitalism as a *system* – that is an inter-related system of economic, political, cultural and social spheres. Rather they concentrated upon important footnotes to the workings of modern capitalism – the need for workers in the expanding city of Berlin, which brought migrant labour into that city, was not central in Simmel's work, for example. The analysis of consumption among the affluent leisure class in the United States, in Veblen's work, did not lead him to investigate, in any great detail, the sources of the wealth of the leisure class.

The new capitalist entrepreneurs generated their wealth from the profits of their enterprises. Families owned shares in the companies they had built up, or inherited, and derived dividends from these. The workers in the factories, shops and transport systems earned wages. The level of wages was fixed, in theory, by the market. The greater the number of workers seeking work, the lower the wage the employer could pay. But a low wage economy can produce a depression, or slump, because in such a situation there are not sufficient people with enough surplus cash to buy the goods and services being produced. Henry Ford, the American car manufacturer, achieved what might be called a major transformation in the development of western capitalism when he manufactured the first cars which had been *mass produced* for the ordinary family. Ford paid high wages to workers, and aimed to sell cars to working-class families. This marked a shift towards mass production and mass consumption in the United States in the early decades of the twentieth century. This shift was termed 'Fordism' by Gramsci – a term which has remained in later social science (Gramsci, 1971).

In 'Fordism' the products were aimed at an emerging, undifferentiated mass market of consumers (Harvey, 1989). The methods of mass production, which were begun by Henry Ford in his plant manufacturing motor cars in Highland Park, Detroit, USA, in 1910–1914, combined moving assembly lines, specialised machinery, high wages to a large work-force and low-cost products. (The scale of the assembly-line manufacturing process was large compared with the manufacture of machine-made cotton Marx and Engels had in mind in the mid-nineteenth century.) Henry Ford's production process was one of continuous flow on an assembly line, which entailed a standardised product being produced for a mass consumer market. Consumers of the first Ford cars had little choice of colour, however, in the early period – black, black or black (Allen, 1992).

The degree to which these methods of mass production and mass consumption, which emerged between the 1880s and the 1920s, can be seen as typical of a whole period of the twentieth century, termed 'Fordism', has been debated. There are debatable issues too concerning whether mass production and mass consumption developed in Britain as it did in the United States, even in the post-Second World War boom period. Britain did not match the United States in the adoption of 'Fordism', it has been argued. Crucially, in boom conditions, Britain has had a propensity to import consumer goods on a scale which has produced a series of balance of payments crises as the British import more goods than they export (Jessop, 1989). In the period since the 1950s this has been most noticeable in the ever increasing propensity of British consumers to buy French, German, Italian and Japanese cars. American-owned Ford, however, sold most cars in the British market during the 1970s and 1980s, cars which had been largely manufactured in Britain. In the early 1990s, Ford was in difficulty in Britain, selling fewer cars and having to compete with more efficient car makers.

It was not until the mid-twentieth century that mass consumption became of central importance to modern capitalism in Europe, although the United States had started on the road to mass consumption a little earlier. It is to the part that consumption played in the social development of western capitalism in the period after the ending of the Second World War that we now turn.

LATER DEVELOPMENTS

By the 1950s, following a pattern already established in the United States, first in Britain, then in the rest of Western Europe, 'mass consumption', in a recognisably modern sense, began to develop among all but the very poorest groups. Groups which had to do paid work of various kinds, from mining to typing, unlike the leisure class considered above, who had to do little if any paid work, became 'consumers' too. That is, they had sufficient income to provide for their basic needs and had developed an awareness of new objects, such as television sets and cars, and experiences, such as holidays in Spain, which they could afford to buy. The older age group, that is those over retirement age, may have remained immune to the new forms of consumption either because they were poor, or because they had not been socialised in such a way that they responded to advertisements and the new social pressures to become conspicuous consumers, or for a mixture of such reasons.

New groups of consumers emerged in this period of 'Fordist' mass production and mass consumption, who began to exercise choice in what they bought. Brand images were established by advertisements for everything from the infamous soap powders to cars, drinks, cigarettes, clothing and kitchen equipment. It was young men and women, who still lived with their parents, but had reasonably well-paid jobs, who formed the first group of specifically targeted and differentiated consumers, followed by women who took on paid work in order to be able to buy extras – the new consumer durables as well as new types of foodstuffs, including such 'novelties' as frozen fish fingers and take-away curries.

It was among these younger groups, rather than married men who worked in manufacturing, or basic extractive industries, that a more differentiated type of consumer was seen to emerge. Those working in the mass media, in advertising, and indeed most sociologists, continued to perceive the new consumers in terms of *occupational class*, however. This marks this 'Fordist' period as 'modern' rather than post-modern. Market researchers, for example, used a classificatory system containing five, six or seven social class categories based upon the occupation of the male head of household. (An example of one such classification is given below.)

Occupational class was seen as affecting consumption patterns in two major ways. First, income level was seen as important. The stratification system, however, was not based only upon level of income. Some occupations were placed higher in the stratification system than others, even though in any given year the income level of most in a specific occupational grouping might have been lower than a category below, because some occupations carried higher social status than others. The higher status of an occupation might have been related to educational qualifications, although people in such occupations might earn less than some manual workers in car factories or in coal mines. From the point of view of advertisers and market researchers, such educational levels mattered because they affected consumption patterns.

To take one example – popular music records. Just after the end of the Second World War, popular music was purchased as sheet music, for playing on the home piano, or on easily breakable 78 rpm records. These came to be replaced by 45 rpm, unbreakable discs for recorded music, and the piano was replaced by the guitar among younger people. The new forms of popular music were aimed at young working-class people, who had had little formal education. Clothing styles too differed between the social classes during the 1950s, even among the young. However, the mass market was addressed by the advertising media as mainly working class. This was a major change from the 1920s and 1930s when consumers were to be found mainly in the middle classes, and this had been reflected in the advertising of products in that period.

As economic affluence began to spread among the working class, so the implications of this process were discussed by politicians, journalists, sociologists and political scientists. There was discussion, for example, about whether or not the British Labour Party could ever form a government again, after the third election victory by the Conservatives in 1959. The Conservative Party emphasised the increasing affluence of ordinary people in their election campaign of that year, and they won the election. It was this victory, under the leadership of Harold Macmillan, who used the phrase 'You've never had it so good' in the campaign, which led to the debate about whether or not the Labour Party could ever win an election again because the working classes, who comprised two-thirds of the population, were voting Conservative in sufficient numbers to ensure that Labour would never win again. Consumerism was seen as leading to Conservative voting by an increasingly contented working class.

However, for a complex set of reasons which cannot be discussed here, the Labour Party did win the next election in 1964, with a small majority of seats. Affluence, it seemed, did not mean that the working class would never vote for the Labour Party again in sufficient numbers to enable that party to win elections. Indeed, at the end of the Second World War, the Labour Party had won the election of 1945 with a large majority of seats in Parliament, and that had led to a debate about whether the Conservatives could ever win again, given the large size of the working class (Gamble, 1981: Chapter 3). Since the period of alternating Conservative and Labour governments in the 1960s and 1970s, the debates about whether one party or the other would disappear, lapsed, only to be resuscitated in the 1980s when the Conservatives, led by Mrs Thatcher, won three consecutive elections. Mr Major won a fourth Conservative term in 1992. There were signs of a need for radical rethinking by the Labour Party after the third Conservative victory in 1987. (These were discussed, for example, in an influential article by Stuart Hall in *Marxism Today*, March 1988.) Once again the idea developed that the ideological appeal of consumerism would keep the voters content and voting for the Conservatives, in spite of the experience of economic recession for some groups during the early 1980s and early 1990s. However, in the United States, in 1992, the Democratic presidential candidate, Bill Clinton, won the presidency. Some commentators such as J. Galbraith, who had earlier introduced the phrase 'private affluence, public squalor' to connote the limits of private consumerism, saw the 1992 Democratic victory as a much needed swing of voter opinion back to the need to address 'public squalor' again (Galbraith, 1963).

Socio-economic class has also been seen by some social scientists as a determinant of more than income and consumers' expenditure patterns, and as having wider implications than voting behaviour. The wider notion of a 'way of life' has been seen as linked to occupational classes. Such a concept is more than just the common-sense idea that different classes have different ways of living which will affect their consumption patterns. It implies a link between the daily work routines, the household chores, leisure activities and the moral values, beliefs and ways of articulating emotions of members of households (Williams, 1958). These elements can be seen to combine together to form distinct 'ways of life' between not only distinct socio-economic classes, but also between distinct ethnic groups who live in the same social formation.

'Ways of life', within modern capitalist social formations, have been seen as formed, shaped, if not completely determined by, occupation. The occupation of the main wage, or salary, earner in a household, typically seen as being the male head of the household, has been thought of as having the central, if not determining, influence on the way of life of the household members. This was thought to be so not only because of the key influence of income level on households, especially upon consumption patterns, but also because the type of work done outside the home was seen to have effects upon the values, pleasures and pains, hopes and fears, of members of the household (Williams, 1958).

Some research was conducted in Britain during the 1960s upon households, family life and political attitudes by Goldthorpe and others. Goldthorpe and his colleagues argued that a distinction could be drawn between newly affluent workers, such as workers in car-manufacturing factory work in Luton, England, who had tasted affluence for the first time in the 1950s, and those in the older, heavier, industries such as coal-mining, ship-building and steel-making in the north of England, in Scotland and in Wales. The affluent workers were found to be more *privatised* in their life-styles than the workers in the older types of industrial and extractive work.

The affluent workers, who emerged in the 1950s and early 1960s, were epitomised by the car workers in the Midlands and South East of England (Goldthorpe *et al.* 1968–9). They were involved in 'Fordist' production line processes. They were more home-centred, spent more time with their families, doing odd jobs around the home, compared with the more traditional workers in heavier forms of work. The affluent workers watched more television, first in black and white, then in colour, in their well-decorated and well-furnished homes. They had at least one car in the household unit, which was used for pleasure trips at weekends and public holidays, and typically it was used by the men to travel to and from work. Most wives were without a car for shopping trips during the working day. The workers in heavier industrial processes, on the other hand, were not home-centred; the men spent more time with other males in public houses or going to football matches and were typically less interested in home decorating, child-care, or even spending time in the home, than the newer style affluent male workers. There were, therefore, two distinct patterns of consumption and life-style in the 1950s and early 1960s among industrial workers: the post-war, affluent worker in new industries such as car production, and the traditional workers in heavier industries.

Whether or not this distinction was ever as clear-cut as some sociologists suggested it had been, it did soon change during the 1960s. As the older, heavy industries declined, from the late 1960s onwards, so the earlier patterns of life based on men doing heavy manual work in large groups and women doing part-time, lighter jobs in factories, or cleaning work or catering, began to change. Male unemployment rose in those areas dependent on one or other of the traditional heavy industries, such as coal-mining, ship-building, iron and steel work, thereby increasing the pressure on women to find paid work to obtain money for food, clothes, television sets and things for the children. Consumption patterns were, of course, altered by the rise in male unemployment in these industries; basic amenities took priority over the conspicuous consumption of items such as new cars, fashionable clothes, holidays abroad, home furniture and exotic foods.

Those employed in occupations which continued to provide well-paid employment could consume more conspicuously, spending on what might be considered to be less essential items in the household budget. Among the relatively well-paid sections of the manual workers, and among the clerical and service industries' workers, a concern with earning to provide enough income to support a relatively affluent life-style developed.

The patterns of consumption, in Britain particularly, but in other western societies too, tended to follow the well-established social status group and economic class categories. Market researchers, in conducting research into which groups would buy what types of consumer goods, and advertisers in designing advertising campaigns for selling products, saw the population as being divided into several categories, distinguished by a combination of income level, occupation and associated patterns of spending and consumption. The set of categories used began to change in the 1980s. One fairly standard set, used in the 1950s up to the 1980s, can be seen in the following list, based on the occupation of the male head of household:

Social classes

Social class A   – Higher managerial, administrative or professional

Social class B   – Intermediate managerial, administrative or professional

Social class C1   – Supervisory or clerical and junior managerial, administrative or professional

Social class C2   – Skilled manual workers

Social class D   – Semi- and unskilled manual workers

Social class E   – State pensioners, widows (no other earners), casual or lowest grade workers or long-term unemployed

This list of social classes was produced by the Institute of Practitioners of Advertising in the late 1980s, and it was used in designing numerous advertising campaigns. Income levels followed this same pattern on the whole, with one or two exceptions such as clergy and educators on low incomes. Such low-income, high-status occupational groups may have shared similar tastes to others in social classes A or B. Otherwise, the occupational categories did tend to correlate quite closely with income levels over a life-span.

In 1987, the year in which Mrs Thatcher won her third consecutive election victory, the proportion of the United Kingdom population in each of the above categories was as follows:

Social class A	3%
Social class B	15%
Social class C1	23%
Social class C2	28%
Social class D	18%
Social class E	13%

(O'Brien and Ford, 1988)

Market researchers and advertising campaign managers began to use new categorisations of the population during the 1980s. These were based, for example, upon age grades and household composition rather than occupational class. This reflected an increasing perception that occupational class had become less significant than it had been in the past in affecting consumption patterns. This seemed to be most marked among younger age groups. Even older groups, however, seemed to fall into discernible patterns of consumption which were affected as much by the stage reached in the life-cycle as by their income level. The next section will examine some of the changes in categorisations of consumers which emerged in the 1980s in more detail. This will help in the debate about how far a new, distinctive, post-modern social formation had emerged in Britain or not by the early 1990s.

THE NEW CONSUMERS

Since the 1950s, and more particularly during the 1970s and 1980s, new kinds of groups have emerged for whom consumption plays a central role in their ways of life. It was not so much the external characteristics of these groups which were new and distinctive, characteristics which were measured by such variables as age, gender, ethnicity or socio-economic class, defined by occupation, but the internal dynamics of these new groups. These internal dynamics affected what might be called the social construction of a sense of identity for group members (see Giddens, 1991).

The construction of a sense of identity can be seen as a process which may make use of items of consumption such as clothing, footwear, popular music or sporting activities, including being a supporter of particular music groups, singers or soccer clubs. Such consumption patterns could be used as a central means of defining who was a member and who was outside a specific group. These kinds of phenomena were found especially among young people aged between 14 and up to 30 or more. Similar patterns existed, and still do, among older groups who may have settled down into marriage and child-rearing.

The young had emerged as a new, major market in the 1950s in Britain and Western Europe, following the United States which had experienced less disruption in the 1940s than war-torn Europe. Young people were employed in relatively well-paid jobs in new industries and in selling new consumer products, many of them aimed at the youth market. This new market had at first been differentiated, in the eyes of market researchers and distributors, in terms of social class categories based upon occupation. Roughly about 40 per cent of the population were in the categories A, B and C1 in the social class list presented in the previous section of this chapter, and 60 per cent in the remaining categories – C2, D and E. However, market researchers began to change the ways in which they saw the various groups of consumers during the 1980s. One sociologist described this change as follows:

> The early history of marketing was precisely about separating consumer groups into socio-economic categories so that products could be aimed at them more exactly. Modern marketing, however, has moved on from delineating socio-economic groupings to exploring 'new' categories of life style, life stage and shared denominations of interest and aspiration. This is a crucial move since it attempts to describe market segments not from an 'objective' point of view, but from the point of view of the consumer. Far from being the passive victim of commercialism's juggernaut, the consumer has progressively been

recognised as having substantial and unpredictable decision-making power in the selection and use of cultural commodities.

(Willis, 1990: 137)

One example of the new kind of category systems used by some market researchers and advertisers, which were mentioned in the above quotation from Willis, is one which makes use of age-grades as the basis for the categories. These were combined with stages in the marriage and reproduction cycle. In this way, such a category system could at least begin to approach the subjective ways in which some people thought of themselves – not, however, using the same category nomenclature as consumers themselves. Age and stage in the marital and reproduction cycle were combined to produce the set of life-stages used in the following category system:

Life-stages

Granny power:	People aged 55–70, living in households where neither the head of the household nor the housewife works full time. They have no children and no young dependent adults, i.e. no non-working 16–24s live with them. 14 per cent of the population.
Grey power:	People aged 45–60, living in households where either the head of the household or the housewife is working full time. They have no children and no young dependent adults. 12 per cent of the population.
Older silver power:	Married people with older children (5–15 years) but no under-fives. 18 per cent of the population.
Young silver power:	Married people with children aged 0–4 years. 16 per cent of the population.
Platinum power:	Married people aged 40 or under, but with no children. 7 per cent of the population.
Golden power:	Single people, with no children, aged 40 or under. 15 per cent of the population.

(O'Brien and Ford, 1988: 298–9)

This category system covers 82 per cent of the adult population of Britain. The categories are constructed by market researchers in their role as observers of the population seen as consumers, rather than reflecting, in a direct manner, the ways in which people define themselves. Each category is seen as one possessing a specific level of spending power – that is members' spending power in terms of disposable income, which is defined as the income left after rents or mortgage payments for housing, basic fuel costs and local taxes have been deducted from the household income. It is worth noting that there is no category in the scheme for 'youth' as such – the young are included in 'Golden power', which includes all single people under 40. Gender is not used as a discriminating category in the scheme, although it easily could be. Notice too that heads of household are assumed to be male.

Consumption, however, has sometimes been seen as an activity and an issue of particular concern to women. Feminists, during the course of the 1970s and much of the 1980s, treated consumption seriously as being of equal, if not more, importance to women than production (see Mitchell, 1971: 29–31). On the other hand, some male writers have continued with a tendency to see the whole set of processes associated with consumption as being of less importance for understanding capitalism than production. Such a gendered splitting of analytical and scientific interest in consumption from production needs to be avoided. This is partly a matter of logic, for there is no logical contradiction involved in saying that men are consumers too, and that some women are involved in production, both as paid workers and some as owners of capital or as managers. It is also empirically the case that these logical possibilities are now to be found in modern capitalism. The gendering of consumption should be avoided too because men, especially younger men, have become an important consumer group, targeted by advertisers and manufacturers of many things from cars to clothing, sports gear to eau de toilette or 'after-shave'.

This change in the way in which consumption patterns are perceived by market researchers, from being seen as largely influenced by socio-economic class to being seen as influenced by stages reached in the life-cycle, or by gender, or by ethnicity (not brought into the market research categories which have been looked at above), has been treated as being highly significant by some sociologists. Mike Featherstone, for instance, has written:

The term 'life-style' is currently in vogue. While the term

has a more restricted sociological meaning in reference to the distinctive style of life of specific status groups, within contemporary consumer culture it connotes individuality, self-expression, and a stylistic self-consciousness. One's body, clothes, speech, leisure pastimes, eating and drinking preferences, home, car, choice of holidays, etc. are to be regarded as indicators of the individuality of taste and sense of style of the owner/consumer. In contrast to the designation of the 1950s as an era of grey conformism, a time of *mass* consumption, changes in production techniques, market segmentation and consumer demand for a wider range of products, are often regarded as making possible greater choice (the management of which becomes an art form) not only for youth of the post 1960s generation, but increasingly for the middle aged and the elderly. . . . we are moving towards a society without fixed status groups in which the adoption of styles of life (manifest in choice of clothes, leisure activities, consumer goods, bodily disposition) which are fixed to specific groups have been surpassed.

(Featherstone, 1991: 83)

The type of society which Featherstone hints at here is one in which 'fixed status groups', or 'social class' in market researchers' terminology, have effectively disappeared as determinants of the new patterns of consumption. This situation has been termed 'post-modern' by Featherstone, following other social theorists of post-modernity (see Jameson, 1983). The term 'post-modern', as Featherstone uses it, refers to a type of society which is no longer dominated by the social status groups of the late nineteenth century studied by Veblen and Simmel, nor by those discussed by later sociologists in the second half of the twentieth century, which were discussed above.

A state of flux has replaced earlier forms of stable group membership in post-modernity in this perspective. The status symbols of earlier generations have become increasingly unable to convey their former meanings, as the names of the high-status fashion houses appear on the clothing, and body accessories, which are purchased by anyone who can afford them and who wishes to purchase them. Everyone who has the money may buy top designer labels under these conditions, regardless of their occupation or social status. Alternatively, those without enough money may steal such items from shopping centres.

Whatever may be happening in the last years of the twentieth century, some set of theoretically derived concepts is needed which can help in the analysis of the recent past. The foundational theoretical concept for the analysis of modern and post-modern social formations remains 'capitalism'. Whatever changes may have occurred in the 1970s and 1980s, they have done so within an economic system which remains dominated by privately owned capital. Private investments by individuals or private companies, not public forms of investment by governments, continue to be made in production, distribution services, in entertainment and shopping complexes, in leisure pursuits and in financial services. The concept of *capital*, therefore, remains a necessary one despite the move into a new phase of capitalism's development which may be termed 'post-modern'.

'Capital' remains a necessary concept for the analysis of consumption, of consumer culture, in this period. The consumer goods, experiences and services on sale remain under the requirement of all capital investments, namely to make profits for investors. The category of 'investors' now includes not only millions of new shareholders in Britain, most of whom became shareholders of the privatised public utilities during the 1980s, but more importantly the pension funds of all major occupational groups from coal-miners to university teachers. Similar widespread forms of investment in capitalism exist in the other capitalist formations in the world.

The foundational theoretical work of Marx and Weber on the development and workings of early modern capitalism remain important, therefore, in this context, for they provided the basic conceptual frameworks for the analysis of this type of modern social formation, namely capitalism. Their work will be discussed in the next chapter. This will be followed by a brief analysis of the relevance of the concept of symbols, or collective representations, in Durkheim, and the notion of unconscious meanings in Freud. These are relevant ideas for deepening our understanding of how identities are socially constructed and maintained by individuals. These earlier writers remain relevant to later developments in social theory, for the later works on consumption, which will be discussed in Chapters 3 and 4, bear strong echoes of these earlier theorists. Older, foundational texts do not become irrelevant in social science in the way they do in the natural

sciences (Jacoby, 1975). The vocabulary which the earlier generation of social theorists introduced, the insights, the theoretical
models and analytical concepts which they developed, have
entered into western culture and have become a component part
of later analyses of modern and post-modern conditions, albeit
changed in sometimes fundamental ways, as will be seen later.

2

Theorising consumption

There can be no theory-neutral language which can be used to describe consumption in a social formation. Some concepts of periodization, for instance, are necessary so that, as has already been indicated, 'consumption' changed from its meaning in early capitalism to its role in late twentieth-century capitalism. The meaning of the concept of consumption changes and varies depending upon its use within different overall theoretical perspectives and, within one perspective, the meaning of the term may change depending upon the historical period being analysed.

To understand the role that consumption plays in late twentieth-century capitalism, therefore, it is necessary to root the concept of consumption in a wider social theoretical framework, one which has been derived from the analysis of earlier forms of capitalism. Consumption of goods and services takes place in the context of an economic system oriented to making profits and of specific cultures which have been *differentially* influenced by Protestantism or Catholicism in Western Europe and in North America.

Consumption, therefore, has to be seen as taking place within the context of the mode of production of industrial capitalism.

However, the part played by cultural values and by symbols is important in analysing consumption if a crude, one-sided, economistic approach is to be avoided. There is no way of avoiding the central importance of the concept of capitalism as the mode of production and, it might be added, the associated mode of consumption, for the primary aim of capitalism as an economic and financial system is to make profits upon invested capital.

Consumption has been a crucial component in the way in which modern capitalism has been sustained, for the simple and obvious reason that, unless products could be sold in return for money, there would be no profits. Capital, which is invested in productive industry, requires a return on the investment, a return which can only be derived from the sale of goods and services at a profit. There is obviously no point in producing unless something is consumed and profits are generated thereby.

PRODUCTION AND COMMODITIES

Marx's analytical concepts have remained as an intellectual foundation for the analysis of modern capitalism – despite the many criticisms which have been made of his work. Karl Marx (1818–83) provided both a theoretical model for the analysis of industrial capitalism and a specific application of this model to the development of capitalism, up until about 1880. Consumption, as it has developed in late twentieth-century capitalism, was, of course, unknown to his generation.

Modern consumption could be seen as a development of what Marx had called 'commodity production' but at a quantitatively higher level than Marx had ever envisaged. Indeed, the amount and variety of commodities being sold and consumed is now so great that it is possible to say that capitalism has undergone a *qualitative* change, that is a change in kind, since Marx died. If this proposition were to be accepted, it would imply that there is now a new and distinct form of capitalism in the world, based on the ever increasing production of new commodities for consumption. This new type may be termed 'consumer capitalism'.

The production of *commodities* was the distinctive feature of capitalism as a mode of production for Marx, but it was the processes associated with their production, rather than with their consumption, which were the centre of his attention. A commodity was defined by Marx as a product that had not been manufactured for direct use and consumption, but for sale in the market. This contrasted with the situation which had occurred in feudal agricultural forms of production, for example, where goods were produced typically for immediate consumption and use, not for sale for profits in the market place. The products of modern capitalism are sold as commodities, in exchange for money, in a global market. (See Bottomore and Rubel, Part 3, Chapter 1, 1971: 137–54.)

Capital, the central concept for any analysis of modern capitalism, is an abstract concept, not simply a concrete group of people, the capitalists. Capital is invested in machinery and buildings to produce goods and services which consumers purchase. From the money spent on purchasing goods by a firm's customers, some profit may be generated as long as the price paid for the items of consumption is greater than the total costs of their production and distribution. This source of profit is in addition to any that may be made from the 'exploitation' of labour, that is paying members of the labour force less than the value of the goods or services which they produce. These circumstances of production lead to a situation which Marx described as the 'alienation' of labour. The concept of alienation has been seen by some later commentators (e.g. Meszaros, 1970) as fundamental to Marx's analysis of capitalism, including the process of consumption, as will be shown later in this chapter.

There is a way of reading Marx which avoids the sterile debate about whether or not his early writings, especially those on alienation in the *Economic and Philosophic Manuscripts of 1844*, are to be treated as being less scientific than most of his later writings, as Althusser claimed (Althusser, 1969). The concept of alienation, or estrangement, does have a role in Marx's theory of capitalism – the foundational form of alienation being that of capital. The concept of capital includes the idea that value is stored in money, in savings bonds or in shares. This 'value', Marx argued, represented in a monetary form the past work of the proletariat. Without the extraction of a surplus from the work of those employed in a capitalist enterprise, there would be no profit on the investments made in industrial production. This extraction of surplus value from workers lay at the root of the objective alienation of workers from the products of their labour in Marx's view (Bottomore and Rubel, Part 3, 1971: 155–209).

An additional form of alienation in industrial capitalism stems from the way in which the products of labour do not legally belong to the workers who produce them, as they once may have done in earlier modes of production. Workers in industrial capitalism produce goods which do not belong to them, with tools and machinery which do not belong to them either (Marx, 1959: 67–84; i.e. section on 'Estranged Labour'). In these ways the foundations for an alienated form of consumption were laid. Members of the proletariat have to purchase the goods which they, or other workers, have produced. They do this from cash derived from their money wages or salaries, or by borrowing against future earnings. They are, in this way, forced to become 'consumers'.

Why had modern capitalism as a mode of production of commodities developed in some parts of the world and not in others? To answer this question involves looking briefly at the early modern period of western history, from the seventeenth century onwards. To understand why modern, rational capitalism arose, in the first instance, in North Western Europe and in North America, rather than elsewhere, it is important to include the cultural differences between these social formations and others. To do this, some of the sociological concepts of Max Weber, whose work was mentioned in Chapter 1, will be used in the next section of this chapter as a means of providing a comparative cultural dimension to the understanding of the development of modern capitalism and consumption processes within it.

CULTURAL VALUES

Modern industrial, commercial and financial capitalism, which had developed first in the social formations of North Western Europe, including Britain, and in the North East of America, was seen by Weber as a 'rational' form of economic action. By 'rational' Weber meant that technically efficient means of production were used, in place of more inefficient, traditional methods and that systematic accounting procedures, in the form of 'book-keeping', as it was once called, were introduced in capitalist enterprises (Weber, 1971). Rational forms of action also characterised the commercial organisations which emerged to sell goods and services to consumers.

Weber's sociological problematic sought to understand why modern, rational capitalism had developed in the specific parts of the world when and where it did. He argued that many of the material factors found in North Western Europe, where modern rational forms of capitalism had first developed, were also to be found in other periods of history, in other civilisations. China and India had experienced periods in the past, as had Ancient Rome and feudal Europe, in which some of the major material factors necessary for the development of capitalism were present. These factors included items such as surplus wealth among an urban population, to act as a base of consumers and investors; a money system; a legal system based upon written and codified laws; mathematics; some science and technology, especially in transport and manufacturing; a state system of administration, that is a 'rational' bureaucracy; and armed forces, under central political control, who could patrol effectively a given territory, so that peaceful trading patterns could become established.

These were necessary but not sufficient conditions for modern capitalism to develop, on Weber's view. It was a cultural factor which Weber identified as the extra ingredient which had been present in parts of Europe, and which seemed to be necessary in addition to the various material and historical factors mentioned above. This cultural factor was a set of values which provided a group of people with the motivation to work hard to build up an enterprise, to re-invest in it, but crucially *not to consume* the surplus value, the profits, in luxurious living. The religious ethic of Calvinism had provided this rationally ordered set of values among the early bourgeois capitalists as mentioned above. This had, in turn, enabled the new capitalist system to become established in the seventeenth and eighteenth centuries. No world-view other than Calvinism had provided a value system which encouraged such asceticism among laity working in business or in agriculture (Gerth and Wright Mills, 1970: Parts III and IV).

Catholicism, for example, had encouraged forms of monastic asceticism in which monks and nuns lived rationally ordered lives, but this had been for an elite with a special vocation, not for the ordinary laity. Calvinism, uniquely, had developed an ethic for the laity who were called to lead well-ordered lives in everyday activities. This form of cultural value system was called by Weber 'inner-worldly asceticism', that is a form of active mastery over the material world, the self (including a person's own body) and other people. This was not to be pursued, however, in a monastery or convent (which would be what Weber termed 'other-worldly asceticism'). The Calvinist type of ascetic ethic was for people who worked in occupations in-the-world (a better term in English than the usual translation 'inner-worldly'). It was a unique ethic, Weber claimed, one which did not exist in other major world religions (Weber, 1915 in Gerth and Wright Mills, 1970: 267–301, i.e. Part III, Chapter XI).

The first puritan capitalists worked hard; their businesses prospered; they lived by an ethic of hard work, with little expenditure on luxuries, which were seen as being highly suspect, in any case, even as being frequently the work of the devil. Crucially for the future development of capitalism, and uniquely in world history, they re-invested the surplus profits which they made in their enterprises, rather than spending the surplus they had generated upon luxuries, as had other wealthy groups in earlier modes of production.

The customers of these early capitalists were found among other groups, specifically the landed aristocracy, and even among some of the clergy in the established church. These became the first consumers of the products of the Calvinist entrepreneurs (Campbell, 1987). This issue of who the first consumers of the products of the early capitalists were, and what values they held, will be explored below.

The early Calvinist capitalists themselves became successful entrepreneurs because they lived by an ethic which *limited* their patterns of consumption. They saved and invested the surplus from their enterprises rather than spending it. This was important because for economic take-off to be possible in a social formation there needs to be one generation, or more, which is motivated to work hard, but which does not consume the surplus. Rather the surplus must be re-invested for future growth and further economic development. Consumption must be postponed. It is this which has proved so difficult to achieve in many social formations in the later twentieth century. Few social formations can now generate and maintain a sufficiently long period during which consumption is delayed and the surplus is re-invested for future growth. To do this there would need to be an equivalent to the Calvinist ethic, not just of hard work, but of delaying consumption, among significant groups of people in the population.

The analysis which Weber provided of the importance of cultural values in the development of modern capitalism is best seen as an *addition to*, rather than a complete *replacement of*, Marx's analysis. The two approaches are not in logical contradiction to one another, nor are they logical contraries, as both Parsons and some dogmatic Marxists have assumed in rejecting the links between Marx and Weber. Rather they are complementary to one another. Weber's work may be read as a development, or a refinement, of Marx's theoretically constructed object 'capitalism'.

Economic actions, such as the rational pursuit of profits by making and selling commodities for a market, as well as consumers' desires and ability to purchase such goods and services as modern capitalism provides, take place in a wider social, cultural context. They are never 'pure' economic acts or decisions, as the model of the rational economic actor assumed by classical liberal economic theory asserts. Both Marx and Weber sought to emphasise this point, that the economic activities of production and consumption take place in a cultural context. Weber wrote at the end of *The Protestant Ethic and the Spirit of Capitalism*: 'it is, of course, not my aim to substitute for a one-sided materialistic an equally one-sided spiritualistic causal interpretation of culture and of history' (Weber, 1971: 183).

Having seen, therefore, that there is a cultural factor involved in explaining why rational capitalism arose when and where it did, we are in a better position to proceed to examine further how a Gramscian approach to consumption in capitalism might be developed. To do this will involve being clear, first of all, that there is a philosophical and sociological aspect to Marxism upon which any economic analysis rests. This philosophical and sociological aspect provides a basis from which an analysis of some aspects of consumption in modern capitalism might be developed.

ALIENATION AND CONSUMPTION

It is important to distinguish Marxism as a socio-economic theory, on the one hand, from Marxism-Leninism as a political ideology of ruling elites, on the other. The latter was to be found in Eastern Europe and the Soviet Union until the changes of 1989–91, when Marxism-Leninism, and the ruling elites who upheld it and who ruled in its name, were rejected by many of the ordinary people living in these social formations. The socio-economic theory of Marx is logically distinct from this ideology of erstwhile ruling elites.

The theory which Marx developed was used by him to analyse the capitalist societies of the mid-nineteenth century. It was what was to come next in such societies as Britain, France and Germany, the centre not the periphery of world capitalism, that was of interest to Marx. Marx's theory was primarily developed in order to analyse the advanced forms of capitalism of his time; it was not designed to act as an ideology of rulers in economically backward countries in which capitalism had hardly been developed on a large scale (Callinicos, 1991). At the end of the twentieth century, the advanced forms of capitalism are to be found in cities such as Paris, London, Frankfurt, Tokyo, New York, Chicago and Los Angeles, cities in which consumption and the ideology of consumerism are most advanced.

The successes of capitalism in delivering consumer goods to ordinary people, to the working classes, in Western Europe, Australia, North America and Japan, finally became common knowledge in Eastern Europe and the Soviet Union during the 1980s. (At the time of writing China remained fixed in a hard-line 'Marxist' mode, having violently suppressed a student and workers' revolt in Beijing in 1989.) The failure of the Marxist-Leninist regimes of Eastern Europe to deliver enough consumer goods to ordinary people, in whose name they claimed to rule, played a key role in bringing about their collapse at the end of the 1980s, in what looked very like popular revolutionary uprisings, produced by students, intellectuals and workers, who could be said to have become alienated from the political, cultural, social and economic system under which they lived.

Marx had sought to analyse the advanced forms of capitalism of his period. His expectation that a revolutionary change out of capitalism was a real possibility in Germany, Britain or France in the nineteenth century now appears to have been premature. These societies were in the *early* stages of capitalism, not, as Marx seemed to think most of the time, at the end of a period of capitalist development.

How could Marx have imagined that he was living at the end-time of capitalism? It is easy to be wise with hindsight. Perhaps Marx and others *desired* to be living in exciting times, in a significant, epoch-making period of world history. Whatever the reason, Marx was mistaken about the end of modern capitalism. He was alive at the *beginning*, not as he thought the potential end, of world capitalism as the mode of production for this historical epoch. We may still be in the early stage, or the middle stage, rather than the late stage, of world capitalism's develop-ment. It seems to have a lot of life left in it yet!

Does this all mean that we do not need to treat Marxism seriously any longer? Given that it has failed to predict the downfall of capitalism accurately, can it be treated seriously as a social theory? In any case it was developed with an emphasis upon modes of production, so is it useful for the analysis of modern consumer society? To answer these questions it is necessary to look more closely at the social philosophy and sociology in Marx's work, not just at the economic theory, which cannot be abstracted from the social theory and philosophy in any case.

Commentators have continued to disagree about whether or not Marx's analysis of how capitalism worked, particularly his concept of 'surplus value' based upon the labour theory of value, is valid or useful any longer. As already mentioned, there have been disagreements too about his early writings of 1844. Are these early texts to be seen as an essential part of Marxism or merely as an intellectual trial run before he moved on to serious work of a scientific kind (Althusser, 1969)? This issue matters in the context of the analysis of consumption because it is in the early writings that the concepts of alienation, estrangement and objectification were used for the first time and these concepts can be used to extend the analysis of alienation into the sphere of consumption. These texts can be seen as forming the basis for later work on the analysis of capitalism (Meszaros, 1970; Cowling and Wilde, 1989).

A great deal turns here on the view which is taken of the relations between philosophy and science. On Althusser's view of science as having a distinct theoretical object for analysis, such as in Marx's case the object 'mode of production', and more specifically capitalism, the early texts are seen as being pre-scientific compared with the later work, such as *Das Kapital*. On a more expansive view, which sees Marxism as a philosophy, in some sense of the term, although not that used in the specialised departments of philosophy in English-speaking universities, the early writings on alienation become important, even foundational, texts for Marxism.

Behind this controversy lurks the figure of Hegel (1770–1831), the German philosopher. Marx's early writings belong to the phase when he was wrestling with various schools of philosophy which had grown out of Hegelian philosophy. In particular, Marx criticised those who, like Feuerbach, saw Hegel's error as lying in the fact that he was not a materialist but an idealist in his ontology. The term 'ontology' here means that aspect of philosophy which tries to answer the question of what there ultimately is in the universe. For materialists, matter (whatever that is at the end of the twentieth century, it did still connote something solid in earlier centuries) is the ultimate reality; for idealists, there is ultimately mind, consciousness, spirit, the Absolute or God. Marx criticised the materialists, such as Feuerbach, for a one-sided emphasis upon materialism in their opposition to Hegel. They missed the dialectic in Hegel, Marx argued (Marx and Engels, 1974). The dialectical aspect of Hegelian philosophy seemed to count as much as, if not more than, the issue of materialism, or idealism, to Marx at this stage of his work. By emphasising dialectical movement in Hegel's thought about history, Marx sought to grasp *changes in history* as the important, central feature of Hegelian philosophy which he wished to develop, albeit in a more materialist way than Hegel had done. Neither Hegel nor Marx was concerned with statics, but rather with dynamics, in human history.

This way of presenting Marx, as a philosopher and social theorist, marks a break (an epistemological break) with those approaches which present Marxism as being a science in the same way as physics and bio-chemistry are sciences. For Althusser, a science had to have a distinct theoretically conceived object, which could be investigated using a distinctive method. In Althusser's view there had been two such theoretical objects in the field of human sciences: modes of production (Marx) and the unconscious (Freud). Althusser wished to maintain that there was no difference between sciences of natural objects, theoretically conceived, and those in the social field. There was no need for a special logic to deal with human actions, a dialectical logic, in contra-distinction to the logic which was used in the sciences of nature. Hence Althusser rejected the notions associated with Hegelian dialectics as being pre-scientific. It was this position which he described as being one of theoretical 'anti-humanism', that is not marking out human sciences from those of so-called 'nature'. There are just sciences with distinct theoretical objects to investigate. Althusser's influential position also included presenting Marx as having developed a science, but not a philosophy of history in the Hegelian mould.

There is a logical problem with all proposals, including Althusser's, which claim in some way that science is superior to philosophy as a way to knowledge. If what is claimed is true, the following problem arises about the claim: Is the claim itself a proposition within a science? No, it is a proposition *about* science. Is it then a meaningful proposition? Can it be debated, or is it a statement of necessary dogma? Either way, it is a proposition about science and a demand that everyone gives up any other philosophy but that of positivism. As such it is a philosophical position, but an odd, if not an incoherent, one, maintaining that such claims as it itself puts forward are not really possible ones to make or to argue about. All forms of positivism face this dilemma, or *reductio ad absurdum*, that if what they claim is true, the claim that 'only sciences produce meaningful propositions about the world' cannot be stated. If it can be stated, it is untrue because such a claim is not itself a proposition *within* a science, but *about* science.

The early writings of Marx, and later ones for that matter, do contain philosophical claims. Not everything can be reduced to being a proposition within a science of modes of production. Philosophy haunts the writings of Marx. This is to be welcomed, not denigrated or annihilated (Gramsci, 1971). *Pace* Althusser, Marx's texts do depend upon a moral philosophy. This is not to be seen as an error on his part, but as an essential feature of writing about human actions and how they could be otherwise than they are. All writings about human actions necessarily imply, implicitly or explicitly, a moral philosophy, that is a view of how human beings are constituted, of how they could potentially act otherwise than they do, in ways which would maximise 'goodness' (not merely pleasure) for themselves and others.

In considering the process of consumption in modern capitalism, the moral philosophical dimension cannot be avoided. It is necessary now to examine further Marx's writings on alienation and capitalism to see what they can tell us about developing a philosophically grounded theory of modern consumption.

In so far as Marx did produce a moral, political philosophy as well as a related analytical model of the workings of capitalism, the early writings on alienation, estrangement, objectification, commodities and money (the cash nexus) are relevant to a full understanding of his project. The early work on alienation, and the related concepts mentioned above, can be regarded as the theoretical cornerstone of Marx, as Lawrence Wilde has argued:

> the general contradiction of the modern system of production, the fundamental contradiction on which all the other contradictions developed, was set down in the *1844 Manuscripts* and the first part of *The German Ideology*. The theory of alienation was not simply an aspect of his social theory, it was the theoretical corner-stone of his political economy. . . . the theory of alienation was also

a theory of human essence, and the negation of that essence of creative activity in the capitalist mode of production was the theoretical starting point of his analysis. This is most clearly seen in the *Grundrisse* and the first three parts of the first volume of *Capital*.

(Wilde in Cowling and Wilde, 1989: 41)

This philosophical basis is important for the analysis of consumption too, for it provides a way of conceptualising the process of consumption in modern capitalism from a perspective which can both capture the processes involved and provide a critical perspective. Why would one want a critical perspective towards something which millions of people enjoy? The point is that consumption has changed its form over the twentieth century, for it is no longer the same as it was when Veblen and Simmel wrote their analyses, which were mentioned in Chapter 1. This means that consumption is a socially constructed, historically changing process. It has changed and will continue to do so in the future, as capitalism evolves. The social, cultural and psychological consequences of these changes need to be analysed within a philosophically grounded sociological framework, otherwise the analysis remains on the surface level. Remaining on the level of the surface is the opposite of what it means to take a critical, philosophically grounded, standpoint towards consumption.

The concept of alienation has a number of components to it. A number of different words bearing distinctive meanings were used in Marx's original German, hence the need for the additional words – objectification, estrangement and alienation from species being. The concept of *objectification* refers to the legal position of the things made by workers. In pre-capitalist social formations the objects made by a workman, or a working woman, ordinarily belonged to them. He or she had made them, and they either used the goods themselves or exchanged them for other goods with someone else, often not needing to use money at all. After the industrial revolution, and its factory methods of production, the goods produced were legally defined as the property of the owners of the factories, not the property of the workers who had helped to make them.

Similarly, in the feudal period, women, children and men had been able to gather food from bushes and trees, to hunt for wild animals and birds, in commonly owned, that is community-owned, woods, common lands, and to fish in the rivers. British woodlands, rivers and common lands began to be owned by private owners during the mid-sixteenth century, and especially in the agricultural revolution of the eighteenth century. Hunting without permission on privately owned land became a legal offence, so that former practices became defined as crimes as new laws were enacted to protect the new private property interests. The products of both farms and factories became privately owned 'commodities' which were sold in the market.

A second meaning which Marx gave to the concept of alienation was the sense of *estrangement* which workers experienced in the production process itself, not only in the legal definition of the ownership of the products which were manufactured. Workers in the industrial processes of the nineteenth century were estranged from other people – from one another because they were in competition with one another for paid employment, and from their employers, and their representatives, in the control which the latter exerted over them in the labour process. Industrial work could not be a socially co-operative and fulfilling experience under these conditions. As Marx wrote:

> What, then, constitutes the alienation of labour? . . . the fact that labour is external to the worker, i.e. it does not belong to his essential being; that in his work, therefore, he does not affirm himself but denies himself, does not feel content but unhappy, does not develop freely his physical and mental energy but mortifies his body and ruins his mind. The worker therefore only feels himself outside his work, and in his work feels outside himself. He is at home when he is not working, and when he is working he is not at home. His labour is therefore not voluntary but coerced; it is *forced labour*. It is therefore not the satisfaction of a need; it is merely a *means* to satisfy needs external to it. Its alien character emerges clearly in the fact that as soon as no physical or other compulsion exists, labour is shunned like the plague. External labour, labour in which man alienates himself, is a labour of self-sacrifice, of mortification.
>
> (Marx, 1959: 72–3)

In this quotation, Marx is beginning to develop the wider philosophical implications of alienation in industrial work processes. Both objectification and estrangement are involved in this. Consumption is not, however, the central focus. One consequence of objectification is that workers have to purchase goods which they, or other workers, have helped to produce, using money from wages to do so. This is not a fact of nature, but a social and historical construction of the capitalist epoch of world history. Consumption becomes a part of alienation because it is cut off from the production process; the process of consumption is reduced to an animal level:

> man (the worker) no longer feels himself to be freely active in any but his animal functions – eating, drinking, procreating, or at most in his dwelling and in his dressing-up, etc.; and in his human functions he no longer feels himself to be anything but animal. What is animal becomes human and what is human becomes animal.
>
> Certainly eating, drinking, procreating, etc., are also genuinely human functions. But in the abstraction which separates them from the sphere of all other human activity and turns them into sole and ultimate ends, they are animal.

> (Marx, 1959: 73)

The consequence of the way in which manufacturing is organised under industrial capitalism is such that people are estranged from one another, and from a process, the creation of goods, which could be central to their sense of worth as human beings under different social-economic conditions. Under conditions of work in industrial capitalism, workers come to invest themselves in the most basic aspects of biological consumption and think that this is where they are being most fully human, not in their work. This produces a culture in which things are the wrong way round for Marx. People should be fulfilled as creative beings in their work – although Marx was aware that there are always humdrum work tasks to be performed. However, human beings are capable of more than just behaving like other animals in consuming food or procreating, for example. They can *envisage* in advance what they are to create. This involves what Marx called 'species being':

> Man is a species being, not only because in practice and in theory he adopts the species as his object . . . but and this is only another way of expressing it – but also because he treats himself as the actual, living species;

because he treats himself as a *universal* and therefore free being. . . .

The whole character of a species – its species character – is contained in the character of its life-activity; and free, conscious activity is man's species character. . . .

The animal is immediately identical with its life-activity. It does not distinguish itself from it. It is *its life-activity*. Man makes his life-activity itself the object of his will and of his consciousness. He has conscious life-activity. . . . Conscious life-activity directly distinguishes man from animal life-activity. It is just because of this that he is a species being. Or it is only because he is a species being that he is a Conscious Being, i.e. that his own life is an object for him. Only because of that is his activity free activity.

(Marx, 1959: 74–5)

The central concept in the above quotation is that of 'conscious life-activity'. Marx was, at this stage, influenced by the notion of 'human consciousness', derived from Hegel. This enabled human beings to create co-operatively with others, according to a consciously worked out plan, as in building a house. This distinguishes humans from other species – bees or ants can build but not according to a plan, not as Marx put it 'to form things in accordance with the laws of beauty' (Marx, 1959: 76). Human beings are therefore, in this sense, to be seen as primarily a creative species for Marx, rather than as a consuming species.

The alienation which Marx was writing about was a social and historical construct, not, as some have supposed, an ontological feature of humanity, that is something found in all societies at all times. Human beings are not condemned to live and work in ways which necessarily produce alienation. Things could be otherwise, so that human beings realised more of their creative activity, their 'species being'. The alienation of the industrial working classes is a consequence of a definite set of social, political and economic arrangements and institutions which arrived with industrial capitalism. It did not exist in the same form before capitalism arose, although other forms of alienation have existed, as in the slave systems in ancient Greece and Rome, as well as in the southern states of North America until the nineteenth century. Nor need alienation continue in the future; if and when the mode of production changes, the form of alienation will change, or even lessen or disappear.

The three components of alienation which Marx discussed in the *1844 Manuscripts* (objectification, estrangement and loss of creative activity) have implications for the analysis of consumption in the late twentieth century. In advanced capitalist societies, the quantity of consumer goods and experiences (travel, entertainments and sports, for example) which is available has increased since the 1880s and again since 1950. Indeed, one could say that this increase has been so great that it has produced not only a quantitative change, but a *qualitative* change, in capitalism. The kind of consumer capitalism found in the last half of the twentieth century was unimagined by Marx, or by those who lived through the two world wars, and the depression, of the first half of the twentieth century.

Alienation may have changed a little in the work processes of modern capitalism – that is a different issue which cannot be discussed here. It has spread, however, into the processes of consumption, for no longer is consumption dominated by the animal functions that Marx discussed above – eating, drinking and procreating. Modern consumption is based upon symbolic systems of meaning, symbols which are linked in with alienated forms of creativity, as in the design of modern consumer goods and the advertisements for them. These issues will be addressed in the next section of this chapter.

THE ROLE OF CONSUMPTION IN MODERN CAPITALISM

In the early phases of the development of industrial capitalism, consumption patterns did not form the basis for a person's sense of identity. It was work roles which dominated most people's lives and provided them with a core sense of social identity as a coal-miner, farm-worker, factory machinist, or whatever. This was the case for the many women who did paid work as well as for men. A sense of social identity provides people with a relatively coherent sense of who they are, of how they think of themselves and how they wish others to perceive them (Erikson, 1968). Work roles were more typically the basis upon which such social psychological identities were built, except, perhaps, among the leisure class which Veblen had studied (see Chapter 1).

By the end of the twentieth century, it can be argued that many groups had come to attach as much significance to their roles outside of the work place – in the home, in sports and in entertainment, for instance – as earlier generations did to their work roles. People now work, in the advanced social formations, not just to stay alive, but in order to be able to afford to buy consumer products. The goods which are advertised serve as goals and rewards for working, even if not everyone buys all, or any, of them. The important point is that consumption has taken off into an almost ethereal, or hyper-real, symbolic level, so that it is the *idea* of purchasing, as much as the *act* of purchasing which operates as a motivation for many in doing paid work (Baudrillard, 1988).

In what sense does the problematic of alienation help in theorising this type of consumption-oriented capitalism? There is still some point in applying the term 'alienation' to describe the *objective* situation of workers in industrial production processes. Workers continue to be hired and fired, paid according to the number of hours worked, and are not usually the owners of the machinery they use, or of the products they make or sell. Whatever the *subjective* experiences of workers, the objective situation of most workers remains an economically insecure one.

Whether or not workers feel bored, frustrated and uninvolved in their work is not the main point here. They can be very positively involved in their work at a personal, subjective level but may still lose their job in a period of economic recession. Workers who are positively involved, and are made redundant, may end up feeling more bitter than those who expected little from the employment system in any case. Recessions do show the objective nature of workers' employment contracts. Even senior levels of management are not immune to unemployment, as the recession of the early 1990s illustrated all too clearly to some. These forms of alienation in employment structures and in the work place do not answer the question of whether or not there is alienation in the process of consumption, however.

Consumerism, that is the active ideology that the meaning of life is to be found in buying things and pre-packaged experiences, pervades modern capitalism. This ideology of consumerism serves both to legitimate capitalism and to motivate people to become consumers in fantasy as well as in reality. Furthermore, it has served to increase alienation. For example, unemployment is more of an upset if houses, furniture, cars, holidays, clothing, or even many kinds of food and drink, can no longer be afforded. The unemployed may lose the desire and the capacity even to dream of consumption. Yet it is such dreams about consumer goods and experiences which keep many people going when they are in paid work, and may sustain others in an unemployed state.

Alienation, far from being reduced, could be said to have deepened since Marx wrote in the 1840s. This is because it has spread into the area of consumption and consumerism since 1950. Consumerism has become the major ideology which legitimates modern capitalism through its periods both of economic boom and recession. In boom times the consumer goods and experiences do deliver, for some, the goal of life – consuming things. In recessions, the promise is renewed of good times just around the corner – patience will be rewarded with another period of high consumption – as the television news bulletins and newspapers report the views of politicians and economic and financial experts who speculate about an end to economic hard times.

The goods and experiences which are consumed have become pre-packaged, already created and coded to produce the required consumer responses. This has introduced a new dimension to alienation. Consumers may purchase ready-made meals, travel on packaged tours, watch sports, television, or listen to music on radio or discs, or drive a car they must not attempt to repair themselves. Modern consumers are physically passive, but mentally they are very busy. Consumption is more than ever before an experience which is to be located in the head, a matter of the brain and the mind, rather than seen as the process of simply satisfying biological bodily needs. In this way, alienation, estrangement, has entered modern patterns of consumption. Consumers have been removed from experiencing a sense of creativity, of autonomy, in many activities by the increasing pre-packaging of experiences. Cooking, playing sports, gardening, DIY (Do-It-Yourself), home decoration, dancing and music-making are all examples of consumer activities which involve some participation, but they cannot of themselves transform the major invasion by commercial interest groups into consumption which has occurred since the 1950s.

For Marx, the defining characteristic of non-alienated activity was human creativity – the artist and craftsman being ideal-typical examples. The arrival of television, since the 1950s, has transformed the way in which time away from work is spent. Watching television has become the primary leisure-time activity in Britain and other western capitalist societies, especially among those over 25 years of age. This has replaced music-making in the home, going to the theatre or cinema, or to social events in the local area, for many people. The removal of active creativity from many people's leisure pursuits has increased alienation by deepening it in the area of consumption as well as in work settings.

Consumption involves consuming ideas, images on television and in advertisements. Symbolic meanings affect modern consumers in buying clothes, cars, discs, pre-recorded videos and home furnishings, for example. It is not merely a material object with a simple, direct, utilitarian usage which is purchased, but something which conveys a meaning, which is used to display something about who the consumer aims to be at that time. Consumer goods are part of the way in which people construct a sense of who they are, of their sense of identity through the use of symbols in consumption patterns (Kellner, 1992: 141–77). It is these aspects of consumption which will be examined in the analysis of symbol and symbolic meanings in the next chapter, before these analytical concepts are applied to modern consumption.

3
Consumption and the symbolic

At the end of the twentieth century, capitalism has become the dominant economic and cultural social formation in many, but not all, parts of the globe. Even in those countries which do not have large productive capitalist industries, many of the people living in them are hooked into *desiring* to consume the goods of capitalism. Whether it is a desire for blue jeans, pens and paper, television sets, radios, cars or to travel in an aeroplane, these are things and experiences which people who are in contact with western media come to wish they could purchase, as long as the basic necessities are available to them.

The consumer goods and services which capitalism has been able to deliver to many people in the West failed to be delivered by the communist regimes in the Soviet Union and Eastern Europe. Yet more and more young people in these societies became potential consumers. Their desire to become consumers, a state of being which most people in the West can take for granted, changed world history, because of the failure of communism to deliver consumer goods and experiences, or even to hold out any hope of delivering them in the foreseeable future.

To be a consumer of capitalism's products, therefore, entails learning a specific set of cultural symbols and values. The asceticism of some forms of religion, for example, from the Calvinist ethic to some contemporary forms of Islam, inhibits people from desiring to become consumers of the type found in the late twentieth century in the West and in the ex-communist regimes in Europe. There is nothing natural about modern consumption; it is something which is acquired, learned; something which some people are socialised into desiring. Once a small group of people in a locality, for instance, do become consumers of designer clothes, certain kinds of cars, or whatever, others may wish to join in too. There can be a state of tension between a set of former ascetic values into which people may have been socialised, and the new search for bodily pleasures in consumption (Featherstone, 1991: 170–96). These tensions may be lived with, in that people can, and do, live by what appear to be contradictory values to an external observer, for example. There are compromises made by some middle-class Protestants, Catholics and Muslims, for instance, who manage to combine adherence to their religion, which may have an explicit moral suspicion of lives devoted to the pursuit of material pleasures and comforts of the kind offered by modern consumerism, with a quite high degree of actual consumption of the products and pleasures of modern capitalism.

Modern consumerism, therefore, depends upon its specific set of values becoming acceptable and comprehensible among sufficient groups of people so that sales of consumer products can be made. These consumption-oriented values have to include those which either allow, or actively encourage, the purchase of the goods and experiences on offer. They involve, also, developing a capacity to understand, to respond to, the symbols which surround modern consumption.

Shopping trips must be made and some goods purchased; some holidays and travel with private tour companies must be undertaken. Consumers must purchase goods and experiences, not simply desire to do so, otherwise no profits will be made by manufacturers, service industries, finance companies or shopkeepers. The global system can support a large number of those who do not buy many of the things which are advertised and promoted by western capitalism for whatever reasons, but this group of 'desirers' can only exist if there are enough actual consumers to enable firms to stay in business.

Modern consumerism also depends upon a set of symbols

becoming comprehensible to potential consumers. These symbols cannot be simply imposed upon customers by capitalist companies advertising their products; they have to tune in with the potential customers' own ways of life if they are to be effective. There is a complex interplay, therefore, between the labelling and design of products, the advertising of them, and the shifting sub-cultural values of potential consumers of various products. Advertising and promotion have to tap into the desires of potential customers, if sales are to be made (Kellner, 1992: 147–8). Such desires, however, do not lie always on the surface of the lives of groups and individuals. They may well lie in the unconscious.

Advertisers and market researchers used to use psychoanalytic ideas in some of their promotional campaigns, and many still do, even if the advertisements are perhaps more subtle than the earlier versions of half-naked girls photographed on the bonnet of a particular model of car. Many advertising campaigns in the late 1980s and early 1990s, for products such as clothing, shaving foams, cars or perfumes, have used the male body in a way which once would have been seen as having homo-erotic overtones, for instance. Indeed, such advertisements do contain such overtones in the eyes of some older males. But such commercial displaying of the male body does not break taboos among most younger groups any longer. Men are allowed, or even encouraged, to look good in their own eyes, and then in the eyes of other men and women. There was a marked change in Britain in this respect during the 1980s. Before that decade the British, under the influence of a form of secularised puritanism, were more coy about advertisements which contained displays of half-naked, or fully naked, male bodies than were the French, or Italians, for instance, in the advertisements for some perfumes, underwear, swimwear, drinks or whatever.

The feminist criticisms of the commercial 'exploitation' of women's bodies in advertising seem to have aided the development of the use of male bodies in their place. In any case, men have great spending power, a fact which shops and manufacturers of goods for men could not afford to ignore.

Desires for consumer products, however, are not all to be found simply on the surface of life experience, waiting to be activated into consumer buying activities. Many desires may lie in the unconscious, or pre-conscious, levels among both groups and in individuals. The full implications of this will be explored in the next chapter, but for the moment the point to notice is that this boundary between the conscious and the unconscious varies over time. What may have shocked, or excited, one generation may become commonplace to a later one. For example, there has been a growth in the markets of goods and leisure experiences for gay men and lesbians during the decades since 1960. These are perceived and addressed by a small, but growing, group of entrepreneurs who cater to these markets in the western capitalist world. Sometimes, the marketing of certain products, from clothing to cosmetics, from music to holiday destinations, from motor-cycles to cars, aimed at gay men in the first instance, then leads to a wider market among some straight men, as the gays may be trend-setters in some matters (Blachford, 1981).

Similarly, markets may develop for some goods and leisure experiences among specific ethnic groups, which then begin to spread among the wider population. This has happened with certain styles of clothing, footwear, dancing and music, which began among blacks in New York or London. It is a process which has been going on since at least the 1950s. It has happened with numerous styles of food in shops and restaurants from Asia and elsewhere. What may begin as a consumer item for a specific 'niche' market segment among one small ethnic group, seeking to preserve a sense of collective identity among the first generation of migrants, which may help later generations to construct a sense of their own identity, may also develop into a wider consumption pattern among some in the indigenous population. Chinese, Indian, Greek and Turkish Cypriot restaurants, for instance, have had something of this pattern in their history in Britain. Similar patterns are to be found in New York, San Francisco, Chicago and Los Angeles. This phenomenon seems to have been less marked in France or Italy, where an indigenous, local basis for foods and restaurants has been maintained. A pattern of consumption which has its roots among an ethnic group, and which helps its members to create a sense of identity, may become partially adopted by some other groups in the wider society, however, in any of these social formations. (For a historical overview see Elias, 1978.)

In order to analyse these kinds of phenomena, it is helpful to examine the concepts and mode of analysis which were associated with the school of social theory known as 'structuralism'. For the purpose of understanding consumption in western capitalism, the structuralist approach has some uses as long as it is not allowed to take over from a wider philosophical perspective, as it sometimes did in the period from 1950 to 1980. In other words, structuralism did lead some into the blind alley of relativism or scientism (the view that only science is a valid form of knowledge and that human groups can, and should, be studied 'scientifically'). On the other hand, the school of social theory known as structuralism has contributed a unique and useful perspective, for example, in the analysis of symbols and their role in social groups. The next section will look at this somewhat ambivalent legacy more closely.

THE TURN TO STRUCTURALISM

The study of modern consumption has been greatly influenced by the turn to the specific theory and methodology known as 'structuralism'. This marks a theoretical break with the work of the earlier generations of sociologists, in particular the work of Veblen, Weber and the early work of Marx on alienation (Simmel occupies a more ambiguous role than the above, having an element of a formalist approach which some structuralists came to admire). The turn to structuralism aimed to avoid two major errors: historicism and psychologism.

Historicism was based upon the mistaken idea that laws of historical development could be discovered as though they were the equivalent of what were seen as deterministic laws of nature. Some Marxists in the communist parties of both the Soviet Union and France, for instance, had made claims of this kind. Marxism was seen as having discovered the scientific laws governing historical change. Such a claim was anathema to the structuralists. Psychologism made a different error. It was based upon the claim that individuals, and their states of mind at particular moments, lay behind major social or political-economic events. Structuralism, on the other hand, claimed that the individual was best seen as the product of the social and cultural milieu in which he or she was embedded, rather than as being an autonomous centre of social action. Sartrean existentialism, for instance, had overemphasised the freedom of the individual from such structural constraints in the eyes of the structuralists (Lévi-Strauss, 1966: Chapter 9). The sociology of Weber was seen also by the structuralists as being too prone to emphasise the supposed autonomy of the individual social actor.

The turn to structuralism occurred after the end of the Second World War, especially in France, where structuralism 'won' the intellectual prestige which was denied Sartre among many intellectuals in his own country (Dosse, 1991: 19–26). Structuralism may be seen as having had some of its main sources in the work of earlier linguistic scholars such as Saussure (1857–1913), and later twentieth-century linguistics scholars such as Jakobson and Chomsky. The emphasis which these structuralist linguistics scholars had given to the idea of underlying depth structures, below the level of conscious knowledge of effective language users, which was seen as determining grammatical rules and the production of 'sense' in language, came to influence other scholars outside linguistics. The idea of 'deep' structures ('deep' in the sense of being outside conscious awareness) which enabled language users to produce sense, and to communicate meanings, without being able to state explicitly the rules of grammar they used, seemed to hold exciting possibilities in other human sciences.

An important development was made by the French anthropologist Claude Lévi-Strauss (born 1908), who applied a structuralist method to the study of language and to the cultures of pre-literate social groups. Lévi-Strauss was able to analyse myths in such societies, using a methodology which looked for underlying structural relations between the elements in a myth. This was a new methodology in anthropology, a discipline which had previously sought to find the meanings of myth and ritual by linking these phenomena with other aspects of a group's life, such as the need to relieve anxiety about events such as sickness, or potential crop failure, or to try to gain success in warfare or hunting. Structuralism avoided such speculations about the inner states of consciousness of those caught up in the mythic and ritual activities of their social group – speculations which could be seen to be untrue when observations showed that people who had no reason to be anxious about anything in their lives, for instance, were involved in listening to a myth being told or sung.

In place of such hypotheses as these, structuralist analysis worked on the 'text' of myths. These texts were produced by western anthropologists observing the pre-literate group, whose cultures were purely oral. It was western anthropologists who wrote down the myths of pre-literate social groups, using their own western languages and thought structures in so doing. Lévi-Strauss aimed to analyse the ways in which myths worked by using a concept which he took from mathematics, that of a 'binary opposition'. He argued that the myths of many groups could be seen as elaborations of binary oppositions – such as male/female, hot/cold, solid/liquid, edible/inedible, black/white, sacred/profane, raw/cooked – which were combined in various ways to create a structure of mythic thinking, with its own set of variations. Frequently, intermediate categories were used to link the two parts of a binary opposition, or such categories emerged within a structure as either especially awesome, holy, numinous, or as defiling, or polluting, because they were ambiguous, that is they fell outside the categories of a binary opposition used by a particular cultural group. Examples might be sticky or gooey substances, such as phlegm or honey, substances which are neither solid nor liquid, and which may become defined as especially polluting, or as especially sacred, in some cultures.

Lévi-Strauss thought that the method he had developed for the analysis of myths should be used only on those of pre-literate groups. He thought that the act of writing down a myth in a sacred text, for instance, would transform the structure of a myth hitherto found in oral traditions.

Later on, however, other scholars began to apply the structuralist method to texts which were written by some social groups themselves. Early writings in the sacred scriptures of the world religions could be analysed using a structuralist approach, some anthropologists argued (Leach, 1969; Douglas, 1966 and 1970). For instance, some parts of the Old and the New Testaments could be analysed using a structuralist approach, which highlighted the importance of binary oppositions such as the city/the wilderness, which was often linked by a sacred journey, as in the New Testament account of the Passion. The dietary rules which are given in the Jewish books of Leviticus and Deuteronomy, which proclaimed that the camel, the hare and the rock badger, for example, were unclean, unfit to eat, could be understood as belonging to a system of classification, or as falling outside the categories of things which could be eaten. This was because to be defined as edible an animal had to have both a parted hoof and to chew the cud – those animals which had only one of these features were defined as falling outside of the boundary of the edible (Douglas, 1966: 54–6). Structuralists treated such texts *objectively*, that is as texts with a structure, but not as authored pieces whose meaning was to be grasped by trying to work out what the intentions of the author might have been. Such subjective intentions of authors could not be known, structuralists claimed. They were to be treated as irrelevant in reading a text.

This last point has important implications for the study of modern consumption, and in the analysis of the advertisements which seem to be such a necessary concomitant of modern consumerism. Roland Barthes (1915–80) was among the first to realise the implications of Lévi-Strauss's methodology for the study of consumption in modern capitalism. A clue to how this was achieved can be gained by seeing the act of eating a meal using a structural approach. Barthes applied a structural method to the analysis of wine and milk (not water), and to steak and chips, in French culture:

> Wine is felt by the French nation to be a possession which is its very own, . . . It is a totem drink, corresponding to the milk of the Dutch cow or the tea taken ceremonially by the British Royal Family.
>
> (Barthes, 1972: 58)

And on steak and chips, Barthes wrote:

> Steak is a part of the same sanguine mythology as wine. It is the heart of meat, it is meat in its pure state; and whoever partakes of it assimilates a bull-like strength. The prestige of steak evidently derives from its quasi-rawness. . . . Commonly associated with chips, steak communicates its national glamour to them.
>
> (Barthes, 1972: 62–3)

The point about this kind of writing was that it operated in an intellectual space of its own. There is no appeal to statistics about whether or not the majority of French people did see wine in the way Barthes suggested – 'a possession which is its very own'. Nor did he offer empirical data about whether or not eaters of steak imagine that they will acquire a 'bull-like strength' by so doing. The analysis of these signs, or symbols, of 'Frenchness' operated by being persuasive, offering new insights and new ways of seeing familiar things or events.

For structuralists there is nothing else which writing could be. It cannot establish the 'truth' as positivists claimed, by testing, or trying to falsify, hypotheses against some imagined 'hard data', for no such data can be produced outside of a structure of concepts. But nor is writing merely arbitrary, for structuralists claimed to be contributing to 'science', to a body of systematically ordered knowledge. However, it is a 'science' unlike that defined in positivist or empiricist thought. It is much closer, for instance, to relativism than most positivists would accept. Structuralism also disavowed the notion of 'reason' as a final court of appeal in what may be said or thought. In this they ran the danger, which some non-structuralists would say finally produced dis-illusionment with structuralism, of 'anything goes'. There seemed to be no control, in the last analysis, over what could be written – for neither empirical data, in the positivist sense, nor reasoning in a philosophical sense, were admitted by structuralists as arbi-ters of the difference between sense and non-sense, let alone good and evil.

POST-STRUCTURALISM

Structuralism has had a tremendous impact upon the human sciences in general and upon two other French authors who wrote in particular about consumption – Pierre Bourdieu and Jean Baudrillard – during the period from the 1960s to the 1980s. Both of these authors were ambivalent about being called structuralists, but both contributed in important ways to what may be termed a broadly 'structuralist project'. That is to say that they concen-trated upon structures of symbols and signs in their respective analyses of modern consumption. Equally, they both helped to develop a break with dogmatic forms of structuralism which led to what has been called 'post-structuralism' (Harland, 1987).

Post-structuralism preserved some of the important features of structuralism, such as the recognition of the importance of underlying structures in language and in other cultural symbol systems. But it lost the dogmatism of some of the structuralist readings of Marx, such as that of Althusser, for example, which was mentioned in Chapter 2.

Bourdieu aimed to analyse how various consumer goods, ways of presenting food and eating meals, home furnishings and interior decoration, among other things, were used by specific groups, socio-economic classes in particular, to demarcate their distinctive way of living, to mark themselves off from others. He conceptualised these processes in a study of France, carried out in the 1960s and 1970s, published in *Distinction: A Social Critique of the Judgement of Taste*, (French edition, 1979; English edition 1984). In this text Bourdieu analysed the ways in which status and class groups differentiated themselves one from another by patterns of consumption which helped to *distinguish* one status group's way of life from another. Hence the focus upon 'distinction' and the analysis of how matters of taste were used in such a complex social process.

Bourdieu examined distinctions between groups, especially in the top sectors of French society – similar processes operated in Britain, West Germany and in the United States too. A major distinction that Bourdieu made, following one he would claim existed in the social realm, was between groups with access to two different types of *capital*. The business, entrepreneurial, management, commercial and financial groups emphasised *economic capital*. Such groups aimed to amass money capital, real estate, factories, shops, shares and bonds. Their way of life was akin in some ways to the conspicuous consumption patterns which Veblen had observed in his analysis of the American *nouveaux riches* in the late nineteenth century (discussed in Chapter 1). However, France, after the end of the Second World War especially, was not as dominated by groups who sought to ape or emulate aristocratic life-styles as the America which Veblen had analysed. 'Old money' families in Europe, France in particular, tended to be less 'flashy', to consume less conspicuously, than the *nouveaux riches* in North America or in Europe. They made use of such social exclusion devices as the appreciation of well-established art forms as a means of distinguishing themselves from self-made business people, from those who had become newly wealthy through some successful deal or business venture. The *nouveaux riches* had what the older rich families regarded as uncultivated tastes – in the fine arts (which they did not appreciate), in food and drink (the *nouveaux riches* had a tendency to eat large amounts of red meats, sweet tasting desserts, and to drink heavily, even mixing beers, spirits and wines), in being over-dressed and in being over-elaborate in home furnishings and decorations from the point of view of the older families. In these kinds of ways social and cultural 'distinctions' could be maintained.

The second meaning which Bourdieu gave to the term 'capital' extended it into the realm of culture and education. He argued that there are forms of *intellectual capital* which are distinct from economic forms. The educational systems of modern, industrial, capitalist societies generate another *structure* of capital, one which was based upon being able to talk and write about culture, to create new cultural products, from philosophical and social science texts, to novels, paintings, buildings, films, television programmes, clothes, furniture and interior décor. The highest social prestige continued to be attached to non-utilitarian studies, Bourdieu claimed, especially in Europe, but also in the United States, in spite of the high prestige of the Harvard Business School, for example. In the period in which Bourdieu was writing, philosophy and literary studies held the highest prestige and status in western universities, in the eyes of many elite groups, followed by the pure study, rather than the applied study, of natural science and mathematics. This pattern could be found in Britain during the same period too.

Bourdieu's approach is one which may be described as 'structuralist' in the sense that he wished to emphasise positions in a structure of access to either economic or symbolic forms of capital. However, he is not a structuralist in the sense of one who thinks that the social, cultural and economic distinctions exist only in the sphere of the symbolic, and not in 'objective structures' in the 'real' world. (This latter position is one which Baudrillard came to in his later writings.) Bourdieu, however, wrote:

> By structuralism or structuralist, I mean that there exist, within the social world itself and not only within symbolic systems (language, myths, etc.), objective structures independent of the consciousness and will of agents, which are capable of guiding and constraining their practices or their representations.
>
> Bourdieu, 1989: 14)

This approach is a powerful one, which does not abandon the fundamental notion of there being structures (class structures, status group structures, structures of ethnicity and gender) which have real *effects* on people, independently of their own subjective consciousness. On the other hand, these structures do not *determine* agents' actions, beliefs, values or desires. The positional structures provide some limits to such cultural and social wishes. For instance, the poor remain poor, whatever their wishes or desires may be, because of their position in the economic structure. They cannot wish this feature of their lives away, in the sense that the structure of material inequalities disappears. But the desires of the poor, their belief and value systems, are not produced, or directly determined, by their structural position in the economic system, as they were seen to be in economistic versions of Marxism, for instance. Such desires, or wishes, have a high degree of autonomy from groups' positions in the structure of capital, without being completely detached from it. Most aristocratic people are not in favour of equalitarianism, even though a few may have been, such as Leo Tolstoy. Some poorer people have thought that the rich are entitled to their possessions and affluent life-style, and have accepted some degree of inequality as legitimate.

Bourdieu was anxious to emphasise, however, that the positions in a structure do not produce unified groups of people who will act politically in a concerted way, in order to preserve, or to protect, or to change radically, their way of life. This was another false assumption made by economistic versions of Marxism. Groups may so act, but if and when they do, a separate activity has to occur in which the members of a group become constituted as agents of social action. The structural position of a group is just that – a position which may be occupied by any specific individual or group as a result of upward or downward mobility. Positions in a structure do not generate ways of life, or symbolic meanings, of themselves. Symbolic activity, including consumption, is a relatively autonomous practice. It is not directly produced, or determined, by a position in the socio-economic structure of a social formation. Putting this point another way, one could say that structural position and cultural practices, such as consumption and consumerism, are independently variable.

Consumption, therefore, can be seen as a set of social and cultural practices which serve as a way of *establishing* differences between social groups, not merely as a way of *expressing* differences which are already in place as a result of an autonomous set of economic factors. There are major differences, for example, between the working classes' modes of consuming foods, drinks, television viewing, videos, home furnishings and decoration, cars and clothing, and those of the lower middle classes. Where the latter aim at respectability, and at picking up cues from 'higher' middle-class groups about how and what to consume, the working classes are more interested in simply trying 'to have a good time', in direct pleasures. The income of some working-class households may well be higher than that of many lower middle-class households; but it is cultural, symbolic, factors which affect their consumption patterns, not income alone, according to Bourdieu.

Bourdieu aimed to combine the concept of social status, and the use that status groups make of specific patterns of consumption, as a way of marking off one way of life from another, with the idea that consumption involves signs, symbols, ideas and values. Consumption is not to be analysed as the satisfaction of a biologically rooted set of *needs*. In this Bourdieu may be seen as having attempted to combine the well-established approach to consumption in sociology through notions of social status groups, with an analytical approach to symbols, signs, to the cultural more generally.

The role of education in establishing this linkage was especially important for Bourdieu. The wealthy industrial and commercial groups, who consumed material goods and pleasures rather than intellectual and artistic ones, began to send their sons and daughters to universities. At first, this was to help their sons attain useful expertise, and for their daughters to acquire some appreciation of aesthetic culture. In this way, the younger members of a family would begin to add cultural capital to their families' economic capital – if, that is, they were successful in absorbing the 'right' kind of cultural capital while attending university. It was not business studies but philosophy or art criticism, not engineering but pure physics and cosmology, which carried the most prestige in French culture, and other western cultures, in the period Bourdieu studied.

That which Bourdieu called 'cultural capital' was not under the definitional control of the industrial, commercial bourgeoisie, but instead was defined by the intellectual and artistic strata. These groups not only created and interpreted high culture – the arts, literature, philosophy, even some kinds of social science, and pure natural science – but they were able to ensure that their definitions of these things held sway in schools, and in the quality magazines. Reading 'quality' weekly magazines, those which contain intellectually formulated articles on politics and the arts, is still much more a French phenomenon than an American or British one. In the latter social formations the intelligentsia have had a negative image compared with the more positive status given to writers, philosophers and artists, in France and some other European countries, during the twentieth century.

Another author interested in consumption, Daniel Miller, who has been greatly influenced by Bourdieu's work, has pointed out:

> The relationship between the two kinds of capital – cultural and economic – is uneasy. On the one hand, education provides a means by which business capital may reproduce its social order. The children of the rich may work in health food shops or other faddish and esoteric pursuits which utilise their educational experience and may provide a more acceptable form of class repro-

duction than simple inheritance. There is, however, also an antagonism between the two orders, as the holders of cultural capital deride money capital as mere wealth and its conspicuous expressions as high vulgarity, while the holders of money capital regard the pretensions and esoteric forms of high cultural capital as parasitic and irrelevant. . . .

Society, then, is not to be understood in terms of a simple hierarchy, but as a continual struggle over the hierarchy of hierarchies; that is, whether, in this case, that of wealth should prevail over that of knowledge.

(Miller, 1987: 152)

It may seem somewhat unusual to see education and the arts as components of the process of consumption in modern capitalist societies, at first sight, but a moment's reflection shows what it is that Bourdieu and Miller are seeking to highlight. It is that the capacity to buy and read novels, to buy paintings, to attend the theatre or cinema, sporting events, musical concerts of all kinds, are to be seen as components of consumption. They require not only expenditure of money and time (leisure time), but also such activities depend upon a set of acquired tastes for specific aesthetic, or even sporting, events. Such tastes have to be created, developed and cultivated in educational settings, which have become a major form of transmission of culture in modern societies. Peer groups and families affect 'taste' too. 'Taste' can be seen as a form of 'cultural capital', in Bourdieu's sense, in that it enables discriminations and distinctions to be made between various status groups.

Bourdieu, as can be seen from the above discussion, continued to work with notions of economic capital and the socio-economic classes produced within capitalism in the middle to late twentieth century. Bourdieu aimed to combine a conception of this socio-economic structure in capitalist societies with that of a structure of cultural symbols and signs. These two structures overlapped within the educational systems of such societies, hence the pivotal role that Bourdieu gave to education in his analysis of how structures in socio-economic and cultural terms were *reproduced* over time. Those from economically wealthy backgrounds were able to maintain their position by access to education in both technically relevant skills and knowledge, but also, importantly, in cultural, symbolic skills, enabling them to compete with those from less wealthy families who had to rely entirely on their cultural skills. There is an unresolved competition between these two groups regarding definitions of 'culture'. The bourgeoisie tend to define culture in traditional and conventional ways, preserving the old, established masterpieces in painting, sculpture, music or literature, whereas those who are from families without expensive art objects, or experiences, behind them are more inclined to accept innovations in form and content in the arts and culture more generally.

The second author mentioned above, Jean Baudrillard, was also a writer who was influenced by structuralism. Baudrillard, however, made a sharper break with the model of capitalism which Bourdieu had retained, a model derived from Marxism and from Weberian sociology. Baudrillard argued that all consumption is always the consumption of symbolic signs. These symbols, or signs, do not express an already pre-existing set of meanings. The meanings are generated within the system of signs/symbols which engages the attention of a consumer. So instead of seeing the process of consumption as one based on the satisfaction of an already existing set of needs, as in classical liberal economic theory, and in some other authors as a set of needs rooted in human biology, Baudrillard proposed a different approach. Consumption is to be conceptualised as a process in which a purchaser of an item is actively engaged in trying to create and maintain *a sense of identity* through the display of purchased goods.

Consumption should not be seen as an activity which is simply induced, or produced, in modern consumers by the advertising industry and commercial interests upon a passive audience. Consumption has become an active process involving the symbolic construction of a sense of both collective and individual identities. This sense of identity should no longer be seen as given to people by membership of a specific economic class, or social status group, or directly by ethnicity or gender. Identities have to be actively constructed by more and more people for themselves. In this process of active identity construction, consumption has come to play a central role. Baudrillard suggests that consumers do not purchase items of clothing, food, body decoration, furniture or a style of entertainment, for instance, in order to express an already existing sense of who they are. Rather, people create a sense of who they are through what they consume.

A person in modern, or post-modern, capitalism is not already constituted as an 'attractive woman' or as a 'handsome man', for example. People try to become the being they desire to be by consuming the items that they imagine will help to create and sustain their idea of themselves, their image, their identity. Clothes, perfumes, cars, food and drinks, all may play a part in this process. They *signify* that someone is *x* or *y* to the person themselves and to others who share the same code of signifiers, the same system of signs/symbols. For Baudrillard, consumption in modern/post-modern societies is not based upon the satisfaction of a set of pre-existing needs, rooted in human biology, beyond the most basic level. In his sense of the term 'consumption' involves the consumption of signs and symbols, not of things, not of simple material objects. Hence, consumers may often experience a sense of emptiness once they have purchased an object which they have saved for, and longed for. The anticipation of consuming is frequently experienced as more enjoyable than the act of consumption itself. Baudrillard articulated this idea as follows:

> This suggests that *there are no limits to consumption*. If it was that which it is naively taken to be, an absorption, a devouring, then we should achieve satisfaction. But we know that this is not the case: we want to consume more and more. This compulsion to consume is not the consequence of some psychological determinant etc., nor is it simply the power of emulation. If consumption appears to be irrepressible, this is because it is a total idealist practice which has no longer anything to do (beyond a certain point) with the satisfaction of needs, nor with the reality principle; . . .
>
> Hence, the desire to 'moderate' consumption, or to establish a normalizing network of needs, is naive and absurd moralism.
>
> (Baudrillard, 1988: 24–5)

As can be seen in this quotation, for Baudrillard consumption is not to be conceptualised as a material process. It is an *idealist* practice. This means that it is *ideas* which are being consumed, not objects. The reason why Baudrillard can make this claim, which runs counter to common-sense notions that when we eat, we eat something which is obviously material, for instance, is that he wants to emphasise that consumption is a matter of cultural signs and the *relations* between signs. Furthermore, consumption, in this sense, is not going to cease. Because it is an idealist practice, there can be no final, physical satiation. We are fated to continue to desire consumer goods and consumer experiences in the type of social formation which post-modern capitalism has developed.

Consumption is founded on a *lack* – a desire always for something not there. Modern/post-modern consumers, therefore, will never be satisfied. The more they consume, the more they will desire to consume. This desire to consume could persist, therefore, through times of economic recession, if not through an economic depression. One day it will all change. But until then, people living under the influence of post-modern capitalism's consumer culture will continue to desire the unattainable – that is the satiation of all their desires.

THE SYMBOLIC AND CONSUMPTION

Bourdieu and Baudrillard had developed their work on consumption, and on the role of symbols in this process, in the context of an important critique of an economistic version of Marxism. This critique had its roots in the European philosophy and political theory, and in the politics of post-Second World War France.

There had been an important social philosophical intervention in West European Marxism made by Antonio Gramsci (1891–1937), in the earlier, pre-Second World War generation. Gramsci's concept of hegemony mentioned in the Introduction – that is moral and intellectual leadership, as distinct from the more usual meaning of the term as connoting the military domination of an area – has been important in European debates about Marxism in the post-Second World War period. In this period a form of dogmatic, materialistic and authoritarian Marxism was seen by many as having been imposed upon the countries of Eastern Europe by Russian armed forces – by military, but not moral or philosophical, hegemony. Gramsci's work led to a more philosophically based Marxism being developed, which came to replace the dogmatic, pseudo-scientific claims made for Marxist theory as the science of history, with the *laws* of history at its heart, which was to be found in Russian communism (see Bocock, 1986: Chapter 2).

Economistic Marxism emphasised capitalism as an economic mode of production which in the last analysis determined the political, social and cultural ideological forms in social formations which contained a significant capitalist economic element. Such an approach has not been able to conceptualise consumption adequately for, as we have seen in the discussion of Bourdieu and Baudrillard, consumption involves a symbolic element as a primary characteristic. As has been said above, consumption is not simply an economic process, but also a social and cultural one.

Economism, in both a Marxist form and, one might add, a free-market liberal form, has failed to allow the *symbolic* a powerful enough role in its theoretical conceptualisation of the process of modern consumption. Although Gramsci did not develop his work in this direction in detail, his approach was important in providing a basis for later work on consumption, in France in particular.

The work of the Frankfurt School and critical theorists, such as Max Horkheimer, Theodor Adorno and Herbert Marcuse, also helped to develop a non-economistic approach to Marxism. This approach had been developed before modern consumption had become well established in western societies, after the Second World War. Its roots lay in both the pre-Nazi German period and in the struggle against fascism in the 1930s and 1940s. In the case of Marcuse, critical theory retained a residual concept of needs, rooted in biology, which influenced the approach taken to later forms of consumption after 1950 (Marcuse, 1969a).

The concept of the symbolic was not fully developed in this approach. It had never been a central concept in Hegelian philosophy, or in Marx's own writings, as was the concept of 'consciousness'. Yet the concept of the symbolic is not logically incompatible with the notion of consciousness; it is, however, somewhat more precise.

The American philosopher, Susanne Langer, developed an approach to the concept of symbol which is useful to sociologists and anthropologists in general, and for those interested in consumption in particular. Langer attempted to write about symbolism and language, symbols in mathematics and logic, and in what she termed 'the non-discursive'. This latter is especially important here for the analysis of consumption. In this area of the non-discursive, that is a type of discourse distinct logically from scientific or everyday empirically based discourse, what she termed *presentational* symbols were of prime importance. She argued that there was *meaning*, albeit of a moral and emotional kind, in the works of artists, in magic, in religious rituals and in dreams, unlike the logical positivists who restricted 'meaningfulness' to logic, science and mathematics.

Langer argued that *Homo sapiens*, as distinct from other species, has a capacity for forming symbols, not merely signs. Biologistic conceptions of human beings, such as may be found in some forms of psychology and medicine, for instance, do not attach importance to this symbol-forming capacity of the brain in *Homo sapiens*. It is, however, of the utmost significance in explaining why it is our species which has come to dominate over most others, Langer argued. She wrote, for instance:

> there is a primary need in man, which other creatures probably do not have, and which actuates all his apparently unzoological aims, his wistful fancies, his consciousness of value, his utterly impractical enthusiasms, and his awareness of a 'Beyond' filled with holiness . . .
>
> This basic need, which certainly is obvious only in man, is the *need of symbolisation*. The symbol-making function is one of man's primary activities, like eating, looking, or moving about. It is the fundamental process of his mind and goes on all the time.
>
> (Langer, 1951: 45)

Langer articulated her argument in terms of 'needs', but her position is not necessarily incompatible with the assumptions made by Baudrillard, for example, who was critical of the notion of 'need', as we saw in the previous section of this chapter. Both Langer and Baudrillard may be seen to have operated with the idea that symbols are central to human activities, and that *Homo sapiens* is, above all else, a symbol-producing and symbol-using species.

Langer's view can also be seen as related to that of Marx in the *1844 Manuscripts*, where Marx argued that it was 'consciousness' which distinguished humans from other species, as we saw in Chapter 2. However, Langer's position is a considerable advance on that of the young Marx because it articulates a clearer difference between *Homo sapiens* and other species than the notion of consciousness allows. For other species are conscious of their environment, and they can respond to *signals*, but not to what Langer calls *symbols*.

Many species communicate with one another, and consciously receive signs or signals, as Marx saw. But it is not some general 'consciousness' which best expresses the distinctiveness of our species. Nor is it just language, or mathematics, which distinguishes humans from other species. These forms of symbolism, language and mathematics, are two very important symbolic capacities. There are, nevertheless, other symbolic capacities which are no less significant. Positivists, including some Marxists, have mistakenly seen aesthetic, religious and dream symbols as somehow of less significance, as less 'meaningful', than those used in the natural sciences, in logic and mathematics. Langer, however, had learned more from Freud than most positivists and many Marxists. Langer wrote, for instance:

> It was Freud who recognised that ritual acts are not genuine instrumental acts, but . . . carry with them . . . a feeling not of purpose, but of compulsion. They *must* be performed, not to any visible end, but from a sheer inward need; . . .
>
> The great contribution of Freud to the philosophy of mind has been the realisation that human behaviour is not only a food-getting strategy, but is also a language; that every *move* is at the same time a *gesture*. Symbolisation is both an end and an instrument.
>
> (Langer, 1951: 53)

Symbols can have an *unconscious* meaning – the main socio-cultural examples being found in the arts and in religious symbols and rituals. Such unconscious meanings revolve around what Freud termed the sexual drives and the 'death drive', the latter being the unconscious source of destructive, aggressive impulses. The latter idea was not developed by Langer, but it could be added to her analysis without destroying the framework which she suggested.

In the activities involved in modern consumption, the sexual may be found underlying some designs in clothing, and in items of body care, for example. These may be seen as conscious rather than unconscious elements at the end of the twentieth century, or so it is supposed. There are, however, some 'infantile sexual', unconscious, meanings which affect consumers' actions, as in some advertisements for chocolate bars, for example. The role of the concept of the unconscious in the analysis of consumption will be explored further in the next chapter. Before turning to that, it will be useful to examine the idea of 'symbol' in more detail here.

There is a confusion in much of the existing literature between 'signs' and 'symbols'. Some of this confusion results from the use of the term 'sign' in structural linguistics to refer to what might be more properly termed a 'symbol'. Animals, birds, insects and fish may exchange signs, or signals, and are thus able to communicate limited forms of information. Some scientists might even say that they have limited forms of 'consciousness'. If this is the case, this constitutes another reason why it is not really 'consciousness', or sign exchange, which marks the distinguishing character of *Homo sapiens*.

There are some limited forms of consumption behaviour patterns which might be said to fit this model of responding to a sign, among human beings as well as among animals. It may well be the case that children respond to signs about foods, or drinks, which they consume (buy and eat or drink) in a way which is similar to, but not identical with, the ways in which animals respond to signs in their environment. However, a child has to be socialised into responding to *symbols*, if it is to become a full member of its cultural group. This transforms even how young humans respond to signs compared with animals etc., for once they have been introduced to a human language a child is for ever different from the young of other species. Adults may retain some of their earliest responses to signs, however, so that they may think of a hamburger as 'a McDonald's', or a vacuum cleaner as 'a Hoover', because they learned these names as signs of the respective material objects.

These responses to signs, which may be studied using methods akin to those used to study biological patterns among other species, are *not* what makes us distinctive as a species, however. To push these basic, elementary, similarities between non-human species' means of sign communication, and those found among humans, to the point where the significant *difference* between human beings and other species is lost, is a scientific and philosophical, even a moral, error. A more objective approach to human beings recognises that their capacity to use symbols, as well as signs, marks a *qualitative*, not just a quantitative, shift and development in human evolution. Let us look, therefore, at this crucial concept of 'symbol' as it is so important for the understanding of the difference between *Homo sapiens* and other species.

A symbol may be said to *connote* the conception that it conveys; it does not matter if the object, or state of affairs, to which it refers is absent from, or present in, the immediate environment. For exchanges of signs, or signals, to occur, the thing or state of affairs must be in the immediate environment, otherwise no real information can be exchanged. Symbols are abstract; signs are tied to the concrete.

The most 'obvious' form of symbol-using among human beings is language use. This has become 'obvious' only since the 'linguistic turn' in philosophy, especially in the work of the later Wittgenstein (Wittgenstein, 1958) and in some social science, as in the work of Lacan in psychoanalysis (Lacan, 1977). This turn to the importance of language has been a post-Second World War phenomenon. Before that, some philosophers and social scientists were preoccupied with 'consciousness', as in phenomenological descriptions of states of consciousness, in the work of Husserl, Merleau-Ponty and Sartre, for example (see Pivcevic, 1970). Others, more influenced by positivism, were preoccupied with natural science, logic and mathematics as the way to obtain 'real knowledge' about the world, rather than concentrating on language.

The turn to symbols – the 'symbolic turn' – has been slower to emerge. The concept of the symbolic sphere includes more than language, or mathematical and logical symbolism. It also includes, as was mentioned above, the arts, both popular forms of entertainment and the 'higher' arts; religious ritual; and dreams. These forms of symbolism are not to be seen as, in some way or other, lower forms of symbolic expression – lower, that is, than mathematics, logic, science or even ordinary language. The symbolic articulation of emotions, both conscious and unconscious, which occurs in these other forms of symbolic expression, is not to be seen as less serious, or less 'worthy', of human beings than the other forms of symbolic expression found in logic, mathematics and science. Indeed, to grasp how language works, linguistic philosophers have found that it has been important to move away from seeing language use as typified by giving descriptions of states of the world. Language is used for all kinds of purposes, for ordering people to do things, or giving shopping lists to someone, to sentencing someone to imprisonment or praying to a God (Wittgenstein, 1958).

No one purpose, or form of language use, can be given priority over others – this was the mistake made by logical positivists who over-privileged logic, mathematics and science. Emotional forms of symbolic expression, in language, or in other forms of symbolism such as music, painting, dance, ritual and, by extension, in consumption, are to be treated as seriously as other forms of symbolic expression in a well-rounded philosophy which is free from positivistic prejudices.

The process of consumption is one such form of social, cultural, symbolic activity, which is not as purely economic as utilitarianism, classic liberalism or some materialistic forms of Marxism supposed. In the affluent social formations of modern western capitalism, consumption is to be seen as a process governed by the *play of symbols*, not by the satisfaction of material needs. The latter are taken for granted in the period of affluent capitalism which became well established in the 1950s and continued at least until the end of the 1980s. It is, of course, not guaranteed to continue in this way for ever. Nor is the type of consumption found in modern capitalism to be analysed in the same way as the satisfaction of basic material needs in other types of social formation, nor vice versa. However, as the western media penetrate into other social formations, so more and more people become hooked into *desiring* to be consumers of the products of western capitalism. Such a process of awareness of what was lacking in communism, namely the availability of consumer goods, played a part in the build-up of tensions and in the disaffection felt with the régime in the communist countries of Eastern Europe during the 1980s, as was mentioned above.

The role of desire in modern consumption is important, for without consumers, or potential consumers, becoming socialised in such a way that they do seek satisfaction of their desires in modern consumer goods and experiences, the social and cultural relations which sustain the economic system of modern capitalism would break down. These desires can, and do, help to shape world political economy (Lyotard, 1974). They are not simply to be seen as the icing on the cake. The concept of 'desire', and its importance for the analysis of modern consumption, will be explored further, therefore, in the next chapter.

4

Desires, identity and consumption

Western capitalist social formations contain a majority of people, between two-thirds to three-quarters of the population, who can afford to buy consumer goods and experiences in non-recessionary years and who increasingly are hooked into the culture of consumerism. This means that many people continue to desire to be purchasers, consumers, even when they cannot afford to buy all the things and pleasurable experiences which they might wish as a consequence of seeing what is on offer in advertisements, and in television programmes more generally. In order to develop the analysis of desires, and how they are linked to the social, cultural and psychological construction and maintenance of a sense of various kinds of identity, some additional concepts will be examined in this chapter. In particular, the concept of desire, which can be located in the theoretical discourse of psychoanalysis, and that of identity as this has emerged in some kinds of recent sociological writings, will be explored.

Bourdieu and Baudrillard, two writers who were discussed in the previous chapter, developed somewhat different approaches to the analysis of modern consumption, but neither of them used the concept of desire in a systematic way. Bourdieu was more concerned with the relations between the structure of capitalism and the field of the symbolic, rather than with the desires articulated and evoked by symbols. Baudrillard, on the other hand, did retain a conception of desire in his approach to modern consumption as 'an idealist practice'. For Baudrillard, modern, and post-modern, consumers are trying to satisfy their emotional desires, as much as, if not more than, simply satisfying their material needs. This is a key proposition for the purpose of analysing the distinctive features of modern/post-modern consumerism in Baudrillard. Such desires, however, are seen as surface phenomena, not as depth structures, by Baudrillard.

The other important writer who was discussed in the previous chapter, Susanne Langer, did develop a systematic approach to symbols in her work, but not to 'desires'. Nor did she apply the concept of the symbol to the processes involved in modern consumption. Langer illustrated the concept of what she termed 'presentational symbols' with the examples of the arts and religion, but not with patterns of consumption and their symbolic meanings. This was a reflection, no doubt, of the period in which she was working – the 1940s – before consumption had become established as the characteristic socio-cultural activity *par excellence* of late twentieth-century post-modern capitalism. It is worth examining the idea that consumption is *a*, even *the*, major characteristic of post-modernity in more detail here.

The post-modern period, in so far as post-modernity can be pinned down to a specific period of historical time – something the purists of post-modernity would refuse to do – could be said to have emerged with the rapid growth of consumerism in the United States in the 1950s. The claim, however, that there has been a major break away from capitalism is impossible to sustain. Capitalism continues to be the dominant mode of production and consumption on the globe. Looking at changes *within* capitalism, however, it is possible to detect significant changes in the last four or five decades of the twentieth century. These changes have been summarised as constituting a move into a new phase – the post-modern. As Jameson has said of 'post-modernism':

> It is . . . , at least in my use, a periodizing concept whose function is to correlate the emergence of new formal features in culture with the emergence of a new type of social life and a new economic order – what is often euphemistically called modernisation, post-industrial or

consumer society, the society of the media or the spec-
tacle, or multinational capitalism. This new moment of
capitalism can be dated from the post-war boom in the
United States in the late 1940s and early 1950s.

(Jameson, 1983: 113)

The notion of post-modernity that Jameson used in the above
quotation connotes a phase in the periodisation of capitalism.
This new phase is characterised as involving a shift towards consumption as a central social, economic and cultural process, and
that capitalism is becoming ever more global in its impact through
multi-national companies. The term 'post-modern' entails too the
idea that social classes are of less importance in the minds of
people than other ways of constructing identities (see Lash and
Friedman, 1992: Introduction). This does not mean, however,
that economic classes based upon the objective criterion of ownership, or non-ownership, of significant amounts of private capital
have disappeared – no post-modernist could plausibly claim that
this is the case. In western capitalist societies, small proportions
of the population, from 1 to 5 per cent, own *substantial* amounts
of capital, that is more than just a few shares, or a pension, or
a house. The post-modern is and remains a phase in the development of capitalism, not a jump into a wholly new mode of production and consumption, or a move outside of 'history', *pace*
Fukuyama (Fukuyama, 1989).

Rather the term 'post-modern' can be seen as an analytical
category which serves to highlight certain features of social-cultural life, features which contrast with those in the paired analytical category of the 'modern'. Such a concept of the post-modern
can serve to highlight consumption as a major social and cultural
process, and consumerism as an ideology, as important features
of the 'post-modern'. This analytical conception can be linked
too with certain trends towards the collapse of the distinction
between the 'high' arts and the popular arts, for example, or
with trends in architecture away from *modern* functional buildings
towards more decoration, colour and the use of features from
earlier periods, such as Ricardo Bofil's suggestions of ancient
Egypt in his development in Montpellier, France (Featherstone,
1992).

Furthermore, under 'modern' conditions, work roles in production processes were defined as being central for identity,
which is in contrast with consumption patterns of action being

posited as central to post-modern identity construction (Kellner, 1992). In this way of conceptualising the post-modern, capitalism continues to play a major role, but work in industrial organisations is not seen as determining the social, cultural processes surrounding consumption, nor the construction of identities.

Such an analytical contrast should not be confused with making empirical claims about the 'post-modern', in which particular features are seen as having become dominant in some societies from a specific year or decade. The 'post-modern' is an analytical, theoretical concept which serves to highlight certain trends, certain differences between one period and another.

An important question arises about how to conceptualise the place of economic classes in post-modernity, given the decline in the centrality of work in production processes for identity creation and maintenance posited in the analytical model of post-modernity. If in modernity there was a conceptual distinction between the objective class position of a group and that group's members' subjective perceptions and meaning structures, this same distinction may be carried over into the analytical model of post-modernity. In other words, given that post-modernity is being treated analytically as a phase of development within the mode of production of capitalism, as it is by Jameson (1983) and Kellner (1992), for example, the objective features of classes remain as they were, but the subjective features are posited in the model as having undergone a major change. This change involves a move from work roles in production, and in activities of distribution, being central to identity creation and maintenance, to consumption practices and aspirations becoming central to the social construction of identity, within the analytical model of post-modernity.

The major means of production, of distribution and financial services, remain owned by share-holders including individuals, families, pension funds, insurance and unit trust companies, and other corporate bodies including churches and universities, in both modernity and post-modernity. In this sense, therefore, economic classes remain at the level of an external, objective analysis. There is a small, but highly important, group who own significant amounts of private, invested capital and who receive profits as dividends. The vast majority of people, however, are in various roles as paid employees, self-employed in their own small businesses, in retirement or receiving state benefits of one kind or another. The model of post-modernity posits that for this latter group, and for some of the bourgeoisie, work roles are of less significance for their sense of identity than their activity as consumers. Whether this is so or not is a matter for empirical research; the degree to which such a change has occurred among specific age, gender, occupational, ethnic and other social groups in specific social formations needs empirical investigation. The issue is not to find out if the analytical model of post-modernity is 'true' or 'false', but, as with any model, to use it to highlight certain features of social, cultural and psychological change. The judgement about such models is made in terms of 'useful' or 'not useful' in understanding change, rather than truth/falsity (Weber, 1904 and 1949).

An empirical example of how the social-cultural may affect a group's action may be seen in the way in which an ethnic sense of identity among the members of a specific group may produce antagonism towards others in a similar economic class position, for example. Ethnicity may also affect patterns of consumption in styles of dress, tastes in music and leisure-time pursuits, or in food and drink consumption, for consumption patterns may be used to maintain and mark out *differences* between groups, to demarcate boundaries between ethnic groups, to mark out some as members and others as 'outsiders'.

Youth groups too, as we have seen, may use specific consumption patterns as a way of marking a boundary between peer group membership and outsiders. Social status groups among older members of a social formation also use specific consumption patterns as a marker of a specific status group's life-style, as was discussed in Chapter 1. All these patterns could be found in modernity too. What, then, is distinctive in the post-modern model?

It is that these various social, ethnic or age-grade boundaries themselves have less significance in terms of consumption patterns than more individuated patterns. In post-modernity, according to the analytical model being suggested here, group boundaries are much more *fluid* than under conditions of modernity; people do not feel that they belong necessarily to the same social status group, or even the same ethnic group, into which they were born (Hall, 1992). They may also move between a number of youth groups as they move from being children, through various adolescent, teenage group identities, and eventually reach middle and old age with a more variegated set of enthusiasms, together with their associated consumer patterns, than former 'modern' generations, who lived within more stable youth groups and status groups. Under post-modern conditions, identities are in a constant state of change; individuals move freely from one sub-cultural group and enthusiasm to another; they mix and match what were formerly distinct categories.

Pop music, jazz, country and western, 'classical' and 'contemporary' music, which under modernity were conceptualised as having relatively distinct audiences, for example, become mixed together under post-modernity. The same person may listen to, or play, three or more of what were seen formerly as distinct, separate, types of music. The British Broadcasting Corporation's radio stations – radio 1, 2, 3, 4 – were 'modern' categorisations. Audiences were seen as fixed in these categories, rather than as zapping from one station to another on a car radio. Other forms of style consciousness in clothing, cars, interior décor, television viewing or types of food – which were clearly delineated in modernity as distinct patterns for specific social status groups – become more mixed up under post-modernity. The same person, it is posited in the post-modern model, may be a traditional dresser and eater in the morning, and go to a pop concert one evening, listen to 'classical' music in the car or at home, and attend a church, mosque, temple, synagogue or New Age meeting another day. Categories of taste, of style, interest, pastimes, political or religious 'belonging', may change rapidly under post-modern conditions; what were under modern conditions seen as distinct, and separate, even mutually exclusive, patterns of consumption and leisure-time pursuits, become mixed together, less mutually exclusive, in post-modernity. Rock music goes into churches; the best champagne is drunk by footballers; pop stars are more likely to be purchasers of a Rolls-Royce car than a member of the English landed aristocracy. The former sense of a clear social status group hierarchy disintegrates in post-modern conditions, not only in Europe, with its feudal past, but especially in the 'new worlds' of the Americas.

The people who were once supposed 'to know their place' in the social hierarchy under modernity cease to think in terms of such a social hierarchy under post-modernity. Style, enjoyment, excitement, escape from boredom at work or at play, being attractive to self and others, these become central life-concerns, and affect patterns of consumption in post-modernity, rather than copying the ways of living and consumption patterns of 'superior' social status groups.

It is for these reasons that the concept of desire features so centrally here in the analytical model of post-modern consumption. 'Desires' do not need to be seen as deriving from the individual's biological body – as in the case of popular conceptions of sexual desires as being given, in an unproblematic way, by biology. 'Desires' should be seen rather as being in part, if not entirely, the consequence of the social and cultural practices which surround people (Weeks, 1985). These help to form and shape, if not entirely fully determine, what a person comes to desire – whether this is a desire to be a monk or nun in a Catholic, or a Buddhist, culture, for instance, or a consumer of fast cars, fashionable clothes, holidays in the sun.

This model is not intended to suggest that everyone is determined to desire what their cultural group holds up in high social esteem as being highly desirable patterns of activities. Only that cultural values, patterns, beliefs, symbols and practices do exert considerable influence; they set the main parameters within which adults choose on the basis of what they see as their best 'desires'.

To analyse consumption in this way, as concerned with desires and the social construction of identities in post-modernity, it is useful, even necessary, to examine psychoanalytic concepts. For psychoanalysis is able to provide a way of conceptualizing desires and their links with the social processes which are involved in becoming a consumer in the social formations of capitalism. The next section will examine, therefore, the roots of desires in childhood.

THE FLUX OF DESIRE

Children in western social formations have to learn to become consumers; they are not born with a set of wishes to consume the goods on offer in modern capitalism. Babies' and young children's early learning experiences affect the ways in which they develop later on in life in relation to consumerism in modern/post-modern societies. It was suggested in the previous chapter that children learn to respond to simple signs, or signals, at first. They have to learn the more complex mental activities involved in responding to symbols, which are more abstract than signs and are culturally variable, as they develop and learn their ethnic groups' cultural patterns. This learning process is complex, involving the earliest layers of experience, including those which occur before babies have learned to hear, or speak, a verbal language.

In trying to conceptualise these early, pre-verbal experiences, some social scientists have turned to psychoanalytic theory because it can provide a way of thinking about these early experiences in a systematic, ordered, theoretical manner. These early experiences of babies and young children affect, but do not determine, later responses towards cultural representations, consumer goods and consumer experiences. As has been suggested in the previous chapter, the central, foundational concept of psychoanalysis is the unconscious. This is conceived of as being formed and produced in babies, rather than as something with which they are born, within recent Freudian theory (Lacan, 1977: 30–113).

The unconscious is not something which operates like a fixed, biologically provided programme, akin to a computer program, which may be supposed to lie behind the ways in which the brain operates. The various and diverse cultures (that is sets of beliefs, moral values and symbolic frameworks) into which babies are born, and socialised, produce different outcomes in the unconscious and in children's and adults' behaviour. It is these cultural aspects of learning which are of major concern here, even if there are some other, more biologically rooted patterns which may operate too. Some writers, however, have even toyed with the idea of analysing people as being more like machines, pieces of technology, rather than being like biological organisms akin to other mammals, let alone symbol-producing creatures.

The term 'desiring machines', for example, was introduced by the two French authors, Gilles Deleuze and Félix Guattari, in their analysis of modern capitalism's psychic structures, first published in English as *Anti-Oedipus* (1977, first published in French 1972). Deleuze and Guattari wrote, for example: 'An organmachine is plugged into an energy-source-machine: the one produces a flow that the other interrupts. The breast is a machine that produces milk, and the mouth a machine coupled to it' (Deleuze and Guattari, 1977: 1). The shock effect of reading this was intended, no doubt, to jolt humanists into a new way of looking at people in modern capitalism. The view that Deleuze and Guattari put forward was that people had had to become things, desiring machines, to fit with the products which capitalist industries produced and which it required them to buy. They would only buy these consumer goods if they desired them. This they had to learn to do from the moment they were born. Hence, the shock tactics in the language that Deleuze and Guattari used.

Nevertheless, their case was over-stated. Babies and young children may be socialised into becoming desiring consumers in capitalism, but that does not make them into machines, neither desiring machines nor any other kind of machine. People are symbol-producing, symbol-consuming, creatures.

There has been an important philosophical error behind both the mechanistic reductionism of Deleuze and Guattari, in so far as they held such a view rather than using it to jolt their readers, and the biological reductionism of others. The same logical mistake is involved too in claims that computers, or robots, could eventually be made to act in the same ways as human beings. The error involved lies in the presupposition that these mechanical, physical, biological levels are in some way more significant in affecting human action than the level of culture, that is the level of the symbolic. If these biological, or mechanical, levels were the foundations of human action, more efficient machines could replace human beings. Given the fact that human beings are embedded in culture, in the symbolic, they cannot be seen as faulty computers, or as inefficient machines.

This is a matter which has been settled by conceptual, logical, philosophical analysis, in so far as such matters can be settled in a society, and in a historical period, which has placed its faith in something imprecise called 'Science', in place of philosophy. The major point in this debate, made by Langer and the later Wittgenstein among others, is that human language and symbols are different in kind from the sign/signal exchanges found among other species. Human beings can exchange signs with other species, as when a dog responds to a whistle or to its name. But people cannot talk to animals about *meanings* – the kinds of meanings which constitute human lives in a rich, emotionally and intellectually developed culture. No dog, or cat, has yet founded a new religion, for example. Nor will one ever do so, for such a complex phenomenon as religion involving rituals, beliefs and moral values depends upon access to the symbolic, which is only found among human groups. Computers, or other machines, do not produce religions; furthermore, they do not desire to do so. Indeed it makes no sense to say that machines could *desire* anything at all.

The reason for the lack of 'desires' among machines, computers, animals and other living creatures, is that they do not have an unconscious which is formed in their first few years of life. It is the production of the unconscious in human cultures, and their bearers, which lies at the root of desires, on a psychoanalytic view. These might be desires of love and hate towards parent figures, for example, which form a sub-stratum for symbols in a culture (Varma, 1993). These 'desires' also affect the choice of sexual partners later in life, and consumers' actions.

Furthermore, neither computers, animals nor machines make Freudian slips – of the tongue or of the pen. Nor do they forget things such as the names of people (Freud, 1904; Timpanaro, 1976). For either they do not know the names of their loving owners, as is the case with domesticated animals, or, in the case of computers, once a name has been stored on a disk, that name remains there, for ever accessible – unless a keyboard operator makes an error in either the process of storage or of retrieval. Neither computers nor animals could be said to be 'motivated' to forget someone's name. They do not have the unconscious desire required for the process of forgetting, unless a human being programmes such a thing into a computer. In that case the motive lies with the human programmer, not with the machine.

These points matter in this context, because if we are to approach the analysis of post-modern consumption patterns we need to see them as rooted in the uniquely human capacity for symbolisation, a capacity which must be seen as being specific to our species. Becoming a consumer is a process which depends upon cultural symbols, and is not merely a mechanical or biological response to signs.

Consumption has emerged as a fundamental part of the process by which infants enter western capitalist cultures and their symbolic systems of meanings. Foods, drinks, toys, clothes and television are part of the early experiences of consumption of young children in western societies. Infants and children are being socialised into being consumers during the very early stages of development. These early stages were termed 'the stages of psycho-sexual development' by Freud (the oral, anal, phallic stages, followed by latency and genitality at puberty) (Freud, 1905). Consumption has become linked with the erotic, with infantile sexual desires, at very early stages of development in western cultures for both girls and boys. These layers of early, infantile emotion and feeling are assumed to persist in adult consumers because they remain in the unconscious, and may be tapped into by advertisements, for example.

The work of Sigmund Freud (1856–1939) has been foundational in providing the basic concepts for the analysis of the unconscious and the transition which children must make to the symbolic level, to culture (Mitchell, 1974: 5–29). The concept of the unconscious was established through Freud's work on the interpretation of dreams, on slips of the tongue or pen, and on psycho-neuroses (Freud, 1900 and 1916). These phenomena could not be understood without seeing them as having an underlying meaning, linked to the person's own specific psychological development. Such meanings often lie below the surface, outside easy access to the conscious mind of the person concerned, Freud argued.

The early phases of development may be seen as lying behind, or reflected in, later attitudes towards consumption. It is during the oral phase that the foundations of an adult's approach to food, drinks (including alcohol) and, by extension, to other forms of consumption – cars, travel, clothing, housing and furniture, for example – are laid. So too toilet training during the anal phase can be seen to lead to adult attitudes toward spending and saving money, for instance. Infants who have been strictly toilet trained, and fed according to a rigid timetable, for example, are likely to be careful with money, saving it rather than spending it. Those fed on demand, and less rigidly toilet trained, are more likely to be eager consumers of all kinds of goods and experiences in adulthood, it has been claimed by some analysts (Erikson, 1950).

Freud's own way of articulating these ideas was within a framework which was developed on a set of positivistic, or 'scientistic', assumptions. His preference early on in his career, at least, was for 'hard' natural scientific forms of knowledge as being superior to his own case-history essays. (One source of the dispute with Carl Jung can be located here – over the nature of science, for Jung was much more critical of positivism than Freud.) The early work of Freud and Jung, however, had been done *before* modern philosophy had taken the linguistic turn, before language was seen as so centrally important to the process of interpretation within psycho-analysis. Freud had produced a method and a theory for the interpretation of dreams, of the parapraxes of everyday life, of neurotic symptoms, of myth and ritual, yet without an adequate philosophical account of what he had done, without an adequate epistemological foundation. This had to await another figure – Jacques Lacan (1901–1981).

Lacan reclaimed Freudian psychoanalysis, philosophically

speaking, from the mistaken positivism of Freud. Lacan sought to achieve this by making the importance of language central to his own account and re-presentation of psychoanalysis. He was more influenced by Saussure, the linguistics scholar, than by Wittgenstein in his approach to language, but the important point was Lacan's attempt to rethink psychoanalysis as a discipline, a 'science' even, concerned with the interpretation of unconscious phenomena, using language as a tool of analysis, as well as seeing the work of the unconscious in the ways in which patients used language. Psychoanalysis had been described by one of Freud's early patients as 'the talking cure' but Freud had not really developed this insight which one of his own patients had had. Lacan tried to rectify this. We shall look in a little more detail at how he tried to do this because the Lacanian intervention remains significant for the analysis of post-modern forms of consumption and its role in creating and sustaining an identity.

Lacan introduced three terms which are important in this context: the Imaginary, the Symbolic and the 'Real'. The pre-verbal baby, or infant, lives in a pre-symbolic world, in which the self has not been distinguished from the outside world, or from other people. This phase forms the Imaginary, the base of pre-verbal imagery, not in any sense individuated for there is no sense of a personal body yet. Later, the Imaginary can be the source of poetic imagery. As the infant enters into human language, he or she enters in what Lacan called the Symbolic. This is the introduction to a publicly shared language of words and symbols, of representations.

But for Lacan, unlike for Langer or Wittgenstein, this entry into the Symbolic is seen as introducing a *split* (*Spaltung*) in the ego of the child, which entails that the Symbolic is linked with *absence*, with *non-identity*. In Langer's work, symbols do not refer directly to a presence, as signs and signals do. However, she did not make this into anything of great importance for the adult's later sense of identity in the way in which Lacan does. For Lacan, entry into the Symbolic is based upon *absence*, upon a word standing for something which is not there, which is missing.

In Lacan's view, though, the entry to the Symbolic does not mean the entry into a shared world of potential happiness, as is suggested in Langer and others who think within the broad, optimistic, liberal tradition of thought. Rather, in Lacan's view, it is only possible to make an entry into the Symbolic on the basis of a foundational *negative* experience. This is that symbols can stand for things, people, experiences, that are not present, which are absent. As we saw in discussing Langer, signs and signals are linked to a presence – some thing, or event, in the immediate time–space experience of the receiver and sender of the signal. This is not so with symbols. Infants have to learn how the symbolic works on the basis of an absence – that the symbol represents something which is not there in the immediate time–space environment. The 'Real' is never fully known, therefore, or appropriated, but it is there, this world of other people and things, graspable only through language, through the Symbolic (Lacan, 1977: Chapters 1 and 9).

Lacan adds to Freud's concept of a wish or a desire, derived from the 'instincts' or basic bodily drives, the idea that a signifier, that is an element of language and culture, becomes attached to them. This can happen, indeed, to the body as a whole. This entails that we do not inhabit simply a biological body, but that we develop conceptions of our bodies, partly through talking and interacting with others, and that these conceptions, or signifiers, interpenetrate and suffuse our bodies' desires. The body is not, therefore, just to be seen as located within biology; it enters into language, into culture, and becomes transformed thereby. Our conceptions of our bodies, their parts and functions, are produced by cultural notions and components of culture, such as rituals, costumes, ways of eating and ways of living our bodies – what Lacan saw as 'being caught up in the signifier', as he expressed it.

Desires, which lie behind consumption, are not simply produced by the biological workings of the body. They are produced at the point where cultural conceptions, signifiers, hook into the body's capacities for sexual, erotic activities and its capacity for aggression (Freud, 1920; Lacan, 1977: Chapter 2).

Why does the Lacanian perspective matter in the context of the analysis of consumption? It matters because it provides a theoretical perspective which helps to link 'nature' and 'culture' – two basic categories involved in the process of consumption, as indeed Lévi-Strauss had implied in his anthropological studies. The contrast and links between 'nature' and 'culture' had been one of the major issues in Lévi-Strauss's work on consumption (Lévi-Strauss, 1969: 84–5). The unconscious is produced as a result of the new-born baby, born out of the 'natural' process of biological reproduction, being introduced to culture.

This unconscious is, in Lacan's phrase, 'structured like a language'. This does not mean that it operates in a rational manner, but 'highlights its non-subjective or decentred character, the fact that, like a language, libido is not the private possession or medium of individual agents' (Dallmayr, 1991: 194). Libido is interwoven with the processes associated with modern consumption, especially in the advertising associated with many products, but also in the consumer goods themselves, goods such as clothing, cars and body care products.

There is one other original feature of Lacan's work which has had a lasting place in psychoanalytic theory, which is also relevant in this context, namely the conceptualisation that he provided of 'the mirror phase'. The mirror phase occurs when an infant is between 6 and 18 months old, when the child first recognises itself in a mirror. The image in a mirror, which the infant recognises as in some way himself or herself, precedes the acquisition of language and access to the Symbolic. It produces, as Lacan wrote in one of the seminars which appear in the *Ecrits*, 'the transformation that takes place in the subject when he assumes an image' (Lacan, 1977: 2).

Although not mentioned by Lacan, it would seem that this phase is not just dependent upon the invention of mirrors, but may be seen as being, more fundamentally, about the infant recognising that his or her mother's face shows that he or she has registered in the mother's emotional life, as it were by the smile, or look of attention, or of love, on the mother's face. It is through this kind of eye contact that most babies become hooked into human interaction, into human culture, *before* they learn a language, before they enter the Symbolic. Babies become motivated to learn language, to become socialised into a human culture, because they have made this primary connection with the eye of the mother, through the mother's *gaze* (see Kristeva, 1980: Chapter 9).

Modern consumerism, which involves advertising images in magazines, newspapers, and above all on television, as well as in shop windows and store layouts, operates in part through the image, by attracting the eye. The significance of this piece of everyday knowledge, based upon everyday observation in modern/post-modern capitalist social formations, is highlighted, and may be theorised in this way, using psychoanalytic concepts. Without some such concepts as these, much of what is going on around us, in the streets, in shopping trips, in watching television advertisements, or flicking through newspapers and magazines, is missed. Looking is affected by the concepts which we have in our adult minds. Concepts and theories enable us to *see more*. As we look at television advertisements, at photographs in magazine and newspaper advertisements, at people gazing in shopping centres, we can see that this is not a relatively meaningless set of activities, but that such consumer-oriented actions are highly significant in the psychic lives of millions of ordinary people. The images, the representations, tap into unconscious desires, as well as desires of a more conscious kind.

It has been argued that consumption in modern capitalism depends upon links with and articulations of meeting consumers' desires, not simply their 'needs', needs which have been seen as rooted in human biology. This proposition appears to be in contra-distinction to the position that Herbert Marcuse put forward, or has been taken to have argued, in *An Essay on Liberation* (1969), for example. Marcuse appeared to argue from a biological foundation in his social theory. This social theory, of course, formed the basis of his critique of consumer society. He was, however, anxious to distinguish his own use of the term 'biological' from that of the natural science of biology (Marcuse, 1969a: 10). It is possible to argue, however, that Marcuse intended to suggest that consumers in modern capitalism had become bound into consumption at an unconscious level, and that he called this a 'biological' process.

This term has caused confusion; it would have been better to avoid it, as it implies an over-biologistic approach to psychoanalysis. Marcuse's emphasis upon the ways in which consumers have become hooked into consumerism at an unconscious level was important, and remains so now that we are through the innovative, but ultimately flawed, structuralist phase of social theory. The Hegelian overtones in Marcuse's work, which were seen as a reason to reject his theory by anti-Hegelian structuralists, can now be re-appropriated into social theory and may be used in the analysis of modern consumption.

Before looking at Marcuse on consumption, however, a reflection on Lacan and Hegel is needed to correct a frequent misrepresentation of Lacan as being always and consistently anti-Hegelian. Marcuse was not a practising psychoanalyst, as was Lacan, but they both used psychoanalytic ideas in their respective writings and they both drew upon Hegelian philosophical ideas at times.

The work of Lacan has more Hegelian overtones than the

structuralist reading of Lacan has allowed. For example, in the last section of *The Four Fundamental Concepts of Psychoanalysis* (1979), 'The Subject and the Other: Alienation' (this being the English translation of '*Le Séminaire de Jacques Lacan'*, *Livre* XI, 1973), Lacan made explicit use of Hegelian ideas including that of a 'primary alienation, that by which man enters into the way of slavery' (Lacan, 1979: 212). As we saw in Chapter 2, alienation was a central concept in Marx's early work. Lacan, however, was critical of Hegelian Marxism as insufficient in itself fully to account for 'the drama of Nazism' (Lacan, 1979: 275). For Lacan, as for critical theorists, Freudian psychoanalysis was needed to help to understand this set of events which had unleashed strongly irrational forces in political and cultural affairs. Fascism and Nazism had marked a break with the assumption of the Enlightenment that modern societies could evolve and progress without the need to address the non-rational aspects of living in societies. This break with faith in the Enlightenment's ideals of science, technology and economic advances leading to the 'good life', has been appropriated by some post-modernist writers. For example, Lyotard sees Nazism as one symptom of the failure of modernity – the phase of history whose starting point had been the Enlightenment in the eighteenth century (Lyotard, 1984).

Lacan, like Marcuse, had lived through Nazism and the Second World War; for both writers the idea of 'history' and the events of history, required theorising, using not only, or even primarily, Marxist categories, but also Freudian ones. This concern with the theoretical understanding of historical events was rooted in Hegelian philosophy. This, however, was an endeavour rejected by pure structuralists (Dosse, 1991). So there is not the caesura between Marcuse's and Lacan's respective turns to psychoanalysis that has been supposed, or even recommended by some who followed Althusser's scientism. Both were interested in using Freudian ideas to analyse the non-rational aspects of the breakdown of modernity in Germany which Nazism represented.

Returning to Marcuse, and reading him as a social psychoanalytic theorist with a Hegelian background, he can be seen in a renewed light, after the structuralist turn against Hegelianism. This turn against Hegelianism had been rooted in some major Parisian intellectual circles after the events of 1968 had led to a move away from critical theory in general, and from Marcuse in particular.

Structuralism appeared to offer a basis for the social sciences which avoided the moral philosophising of critical theory on the one hand, and the intellectual aridity of positivism on the other. However, this hope has been frustrated because the categories of 'human action' and of 'history' cannot easily be avoided in the social sciences as most structuralists had tried to do. Marcuse's writings can be reread in the new situation as important attempts to theorise change in western societies, crucially the growth in the role of consumption and the ideology of consumerism since 1950.

There is the possibility of rereading Marcuse's work, such as *Eros and Civilization* (first published in 1956) and *An Essay on Liberation* (1969a), in such a way that he need not be accused of simple-minded biologism. Marcuse argued that for socio-economic change away from the destructive effects of consumer capitalism to be possible, or thinkable, in the first instance, some modification in the 'malleability of human nature', which would reach 'into the depth of man's instinctual structure' had to be thought about and then accomplished in some way. In Marcuse's work, like that of structuralists and post-structuralists, theoretical work is part of practice; a new way of thinking is itself a part of historical change (Marcuse, 1969a: 10).

Marcuse introduced the idea of there being a 'second nature' which has inscribed on to it the desires of consumption which modern capitalism needed in the modern period. For change to be possible, revolt must reach 'into this "second" nature, into these ingrown patterns', otherwise change would be incomplete (Marcuse, 1969a: 11). Marcuse continued:

> The so-called consumer economy and the politics of corporate capitalism have created a second nature of man which ties him libidinally and aggressively to the commodity form. The need for possessing, consuming, handling, and constantly renewing the gadgets, devices, instruments, engines, offered to and imposed upon the people, for using these wares even at the danger of one's own destruction, has become a 'biological' need. . . . The second nature of man thus militates against any change that would . . . abolish his existence as a consumer consuming himself in buying and selling.
>
> (Marcuse, 1969a: 11)

For Marcuse, a change away from desires for consumption is difficult but possible, so that his use of the word 'biological' is a rhetorical device, not a serious claim within natural science. Modern consumption, and the ideology of consumerism, are social, cultural constructions; they could be other than they are in Marcuse's view.

Turning to look at consumption from a psychoanalytic perspective more specifically, it is the concept of unconscious desire which is, as we have seen, important. Unconscious desires are not to be seen as located simply in the individual. Desires are not formed, even in the unconscious, in a social or cultural vacuum. Modern consumption depends upon advertising and the display of commodities in shopping centres, shopping malls, in a way which *creates* and elicits desires.

The process of consumption into which many people in western capitalism, and some who live in other kinds of social formation outside it, are linked is affected by social institutions, crucially by the mass media, especially television. Major American television series are viewed as being about life-styles, at least in the eyes of many viewers, for consumer goods surround the characters who are portrayed in them, for example. The furniture, house decoration, cars, clothing, eating and drinking habits, the 'look' of the characters achieved through a mix of hair-styling, clothing and cosmetics, create images of life-styles which are perceived as being desirable in the eyes of the viewers. Some people wanted to buy copies of consumer goods which they had seen in television series; others were influenced more indirectly by TV soaps and series, such as *Dallas* and *Dynasty*, in the 1980s (Friedman, 1992: 331–66).

Desires appear as in a state of flux; they are fluid; they flow in unanticipated directions. They are related to sexual potentialities of the human body as this has become articulated in images, symbols and representations in the decades since the invention of cinema, magazines and colour photography, and, above all, television. The desires of the unconscious remain, however, untamed. They can never be fully controlled by the rational part of the mind, by morality, or by consumer capitalism.

Lacan, as was seen above, established a break with an over-individualised approach to psychoanalysis, an approach which had become established in the United States in particular. He avoided, too, the over-socialised conception of man, a conception which linked in with the individualised therapeutic approach in which the emphasis is placed upon social conformity with the 'normal'. But Lacan remained within a broad structuralist approach which led him to seek a value-neutral language, and eventually even to try to state his ideas in mathematical form – a truly structuralist move, for mathematical formulae represent pure structures, uncontaminated by human desires (Lacan, 1977: 302–3).

Lacan's own work was *synchronic*, that is an examination of the structures of the unconscious outside of historical time. But there remains the necessity of relating such structures to historical changes in a *diachronic* analysis to complete the agenda. There need not be a logical discontinuity between the two types of analysis, even though the synchronic should logically precede the diachronic. In other words, the analysis of changes *within* the same set of structural relations should logically precede the analysis of changes *of* such structures, considered as whole historical formations.

Some writers, such as Marcuse, have tended to begin the analysis of historical change before establishing clearly the parameters of the structures of the social-cultural formation under analysis. Structuralists, on the other hand, including Lacan, failed to link their synchronic analysis of structures, such as the unconscious and culture, with diachronic analysis of concrete situations. Crucially, for our purpose here, Lacan did not develop an analysis of consumption as such. What Lacan emphasised was that desires do not run always, nor automatically, in the tracks, or grooves, that a specific culture expects them to run in. This position is one which contrasts with that of the American sociologist Talcott Parsons (1902–1979), for instance, who assumed that the process of socialisation achieved a degree of fit between the individual's wishes and those which a particular society required (Hamilton, 1983). Those who try to live as though their own desires do always fit with what their cultural group defines as 'natural', 'proper' or 'acceptable', but whose unconscious desires do not run along the prescribed tracks, run the risk of falling ill. They develop neuroses, even psychoses, and/or physical symptoms.

Neither Parsons nor Lacan analysed consumption as a major cultural and social psychological phenomenon. However, from the work by Baudrillard, Bourdieu, Featherstone, Jameson and others, on the importance of consumption in modern/postmodern capitalism, it is possible to recognise just how crucial consumption patterns have become in the development of sociocultural identities. This process of identity construction and maintenance requires to be conceptualised in a way which addresses the role of desires, for an identity is not a static state, but an active set of performances which show to others, and to the person himself, the kind of person he desires to be taken to be. A central component of identity, as this is maintained and constructed through consumption patterns, is gender. The next section of this chapter will examine how consumption may be affected by gender.

GENDER AND CONSUMPTION

Women have been seen by social scientists, for example by R. Bowlby (1987), as being especially involved in consumption as a social process. At the end of the nineteenth century, the Paris store Bon Marché opened and made an especial appeal to women in its promotional literature. The diaries which it gave away when it first opened contained detailed instructions about how to reach the new department store by using public transport. Bowlby comments on this as follows:

> That this should have been practically available to the bourgeois lady marks a significant break with the past: department stores were in fact the first public places – other than churches or cathedrals – which were considered respectable for her to visit without a male companion. But this also signalled, at another level, a stepping out from domestic bounds.
>
> (Bowlby, 1987: 189)

From the mid-nineteenth century, women had been exhorted to 'Go out and buy' in the United States; in Britain and in Germany a little later. But by the last two decades of the nineteenth century shopping in large department stores had become an important activity outside the household for middle-class women in the main cities of western capitalism.

In this period of modern capitalism the binary relation of production and consumption was quite strongly gendered: production for men, consumption for women. Production was active, led to men earning money and provided them with some form of power exercised through newly created trade unions, for instance. Consumption was more passive, involved spending money, and did not lead to any publicly recognisable forms of power. However, consumption involves goods being purchased for their symbolic value, their meaning to the consumer, not just for their material use-value. This aspect of the process gave women some control over the meanings to be associated with consumption. As Judith Williamson (1986) has said: 'The conscious chosen meaning in most people's lives comes much more from what they consume than what they produce' (p. 230).

Consumer goods have become a crucial area for the construction of meanings, identities, gender roles, in post-modern capitalism. John Fiske (1989) has argued that: 'Commodities are not just objects of economic exchange; they are goods to think with, goods to speak with' (p. 31).

The period which developed the department stores in cities as a site for women also marked the period which was a prelude to the two world wars of the twentieth century. Women mothered children in the home and went shopping as men went to paid work outside the home, and then went to war to kill and be killed. The modern period was marked by this gender division between mothering and consumption on the one hand, and production and making war on the other. The post-modern has been, by comparison, a period of peace in Western Europe, North America and Japan. This has allowed a change in gender roles for men. No longer required in large numbers as fighters, men, especially younger men, have become consumers too since the 1950s.

There is no general agreement among natural scientists about whether or not human beings are 'naturally' destructively aggressive. It has been claimed that in some cultures men have been pacific; but that in other cultures many men and women have displayed aggression as gender appropriate behaviour (Mead, 1962: 357–75). If it is the case that some human groups have been both peace-loving in their values and peaceful in their behaviour, there cannot be a simple, biological male, or female, genetic impulse towards destructive aggression, unaffected by cultures, which can be said to be the cause of fighting, warfare or killings among twentieth-century peoples. Nor, if it is the case that some women have been actively, not passively, involved in warfare, in fighting, murder and violence against other human beings, as indeed it is, can destructive aggression be seen as constituting an 'essential' feature of masculinity, even though it is the case that it has been males who have done more fighting of all kinds than women. The causes of this male proneness to fighting lie in human social, historical and cultural circumstances, not in biological programming, not in some natural core, or 'essence', of being a male. Masculinity, like femininity, is culturally and historically *variable*. As one recent writer has articulated this:

> People construct and use their bodies, though they do not use them in conditions of their own choosing, and their constructions are overlaid with ideologies. But these ideologies are not fixed; as they are reproduced in body techniques and practices, so they are modified.
>
> (Frank, 1991: 47)

In the second half of the twentieth century, in the main western capitalist societies, men too have become 'consumers'. They have not had to face major wars, which involved all men of fighting age, as happened in the first half of the twentieth century. Consequently, masculinity has not been defined as centrally involved with fighting in wars, nor even with being in the state's armed forces, in western capitalism. The end of the Cold War in the early 1990s seems to have set the seal on this new situation in the 'core' capitalist countries such as the United States, Japan, Germany, France, Canada, Australia and Britain. This may well continue to be the case for the foreseeable future, despite smaller-scale wars continuing in and between the social formations on the 'periphery' of western capitalism, such as Iran, Iraq, Ireland, Argentina, what was Yugoslavia, or Russia and the nations of the former Soviet Union, as it was called up to 1991. In these 'peripheral' social formations, masculinity remains largely defined in terms of the capacity, or willingness, to fight, both in the armed forces of the state and/or among males informally. Consumption, in the sense being discussed here, remains of little importance in the *economies* of these social formations, but this does not mean that it is not becoming of increasing importance in the *social-psychological* world of 'desires' among young men and women.

Desires, it has been argued above, are not fixed by human biology, although they relate to the human body and its various capacities for sensual enjoyment and aggressive action. As was discussed above in relation to Lacan's work, desires are created during the socialisation process, crucially in the entry into the Symbolic, into culture and language. The early experiences of pre-verbal babies, and their own entry into a language, lay the foundations for later childhood, adolescent and adult desires. Although there can appear to be something fixed, and unmovable, about adult desires, it is important to analyse them as having been created in humans during the socialisation process in the first instance. There could only be said to be a residue of a given, biologically fixed, component in human actions *after* all cultural symbolic desires had been allowed for in any analysis. Some groups and individuals may think and believe that their desires are given biologically – some aggressive people, or some homosexuals, for instance (Tiger, 1969: Chapter 1). These kinds of beliefs should be seen as intellectual creations, as ideologies, not as accurate readings, as it were, of an internal set of given desires. Human desires are not already formed and linked to cultural objects, at birth, by mother nature.

The phrase 'the flux of desires' implies that desires are not fixed biologically, nor fixed in a set pattern for the whole of a person's life-cycle, but may change over time. This has important implications for the analysis of consumption in general, and for male consumption in particular. Some consumer goods, and consumer experiences, have become focused upon men, and play upon changing symbols and images of masculinity. For example, some sporting events have become surrounded with ritual and symbolism which involve men particularly in spending money upon special clothing; upon transportation to and from events; eating and drinking; as well as spending on admission charges to see sporting events. Television sets and video-recorders are also important in this context, because many people, especially men, may wish to record some sporting events which are broadcast while they are at work or asleep. Soccer has been the most publicised of such sporting events in which men, particularly, consume a largely ritualised, symbolic repertoire of experiences (Dunning, *et al.* 1988).

Many men, and some women, spend time and money in consuming sport by either being actively involved in it or watching it. From cricket to horse-riding, from pool to ice-skating, or from winter sports to fishing, consumers either buy the equipment assumed to be necessary for participating in their chosen sport, or pay to watch events of local, national or international significance. Even walking involves buying special clothing and footwear if it is to be done 'seriously', and was second only to watching television as a favourite leisure-time activity in Britain in the 1980s.

Sport is defined in western culture as being congruent with masculinity. It has become a large business, involving large amounts of money, not only when soccer stars are sold to other clubs for a million pounds or more, but in the sale of all the special clothing, footwear and equipment needed for participation in the wide variety of sports which have developed in western societies.

Sports have been defined in the past as being a 'manly' pursuit, but more women have become involved with participating in, and watching, sports on an increasing scale in the last decades of the twentieth century. Men, however, are actively encouraged to be involved in the consumption of sport in western societies, especially in Anglo-Saxon cultures. However, during the 1980s, since the development of AIDS (Acquired Immune Deficiency Syndrome), men have returned to a more traditional way of defining masculinity in part by what it is *against* (being homosexual, being gay) as well as by what it is *for* (sport and fighting) in some sub-cultural groups (Weeks, 1992).

Conceptions of masculinity have changed in the second half of the twentieth century, so that men too are increasingly 'hailed' in the mass media, in advertisements particularly, as consumers. Such changes in conceptions of masculinity have been important in developing new consumption patterns among men. Since the end of the 1950s, men in Britain and in much of Western Europe have not been defined or perceived by governments, by businesses, by parents, or by their peers, as potential fighters in wars. This contrasted greatly with the situation of those men who had been socialised under the shadow of the two world wars, for in that period masculinity had been defined in terms of being actual or potential members of the fighting forces as mentioned above. This absence of warfare has led to a change in conceptions of masculinity towards the male being defined in his role as a consumer, not as a fighter.

There was another difference, between cultures rather than between generations, which has affected patterns of consumption among men. Whereas in the more catholic cultures of France, Italy and Spain, for instance, men had been defined traditionally in the culture as discriminating consumers of clothes, perfumes, of food and wines, for example, in Britain, puritanism had been effectively reinforced by war-time shortages and experiences. Men, in particular, in contrast to women, were not expected to be discriminating consumers of such things. Women in Britain bought most of their sons' and their husbands' clothes, items for the household and food for eating in the home – where most consumption of food took place. In Britain, men had a drink in the pub, then went home to eat a meal prepared by their wives or mothers. It was the Latin, catholic cultures in Europe which had a tradition of men eating in restaurants, often before going home to their wives and families. It was some of these traditional patterns of male consumption which began to change in Britain from the early 1950s.

Since that time, British men, like their counterparts elsewhere, have become consumers of a wide variety of goods and experiences, as mentioned above. The Teddy boys of the 1950s were one of the first male youth groups to emerge in Britain with a distinctive sense of identity. This identity was constructed, in large part, around a distinctive pattern of consumption, that of Edwardian-style clothing, a special hairstyle, and a taste for rock'n'roll music. The film *Rock Around the Clock*, featuring Bill Haley, became notorious in the 1950s for the riots which took place in and around cinemas in which the film was shown. Rock'n'roll music was seen by some older people, such as journalists, teachers and politicians, as having a disturbing influence on the young, especially on young men. It was the music, its beat and rhythms, which was blamed for the rioting among the young who had grown up during the war-time period, not the violence of the 1939–45 war. In the war-time period, the news had been of violence and the events of war. Bombs fell on towns, cities and country areas which had airfields located in them. The young men attracted to rock'n'roll in the late 1950s had been born just before the outbreak of the Second World War. If the early years of a baby's or child's life matter for latter psychological development, it might be suggested plausibly that it had been the adults' war which was one of the main sources of any violence in the young rock'n'rollers. The Teddy boys of this period were the first signs of new male attitudes to consumption, and to the construction of a sense of identity through the use of clothing and body grooming (Cohen, 1973).

In the 1960s another major social differentiation constructed around differing patterns of male consumption emerged and was the subject of media attention. This time it was the Mods and the Rockers. Consumption patterns were again central to this labelling system: Mods wore ties and suits, Rockers wore black leather jackets and trousers; Mods rode on scooters, Rockers rode on motor-cycles; hairstyles also differed for the two groups. Each had young women who went around at times with one or other group, as they became increasingly socially visible. The young women were not involved, however, in the ritual fighting between the two groups at various seaside resorts on Bank Holiday weekends, which was reported by, if not staged for, the newspaper photographers and television cameras (Cohen, 1973).

There have been many other groups among the young since that period. For example, there were Hip-Hop boys, and some girls, in the 1980s, a label which began in New York. ('Rap' was also used for this group which had a specific set of tastes in sports clothes and in music.) During most, if not all, of this period, 1954–1990, young men frequently had more surplus income available to them than many young women, for women were employed typically in lower-paid jobs than their male counterparts. Both genders became major consumer groups, targeted by manufacturers, by advertisers, by department stores and by the music industry.

It is important not to conceptualise either women or men as passive *target* groups only, however. The young were not only target groups for advertisers. They actively desired to articulate their own sense of identity, their own sense of who they were. Such an articulation of identity was achieved through clothes, hair, body decoration, from perfume to ear-rings, as well as through cars, motor-cycles, travel, music and sports. If in the earlier period this identity still reflected class differences – the Teds and Rockers being working class and the Mods being more typically white-collar workers – by the 1980s some observers claimed that class had weakened in its effects upon the social construction of identity.

The sociologist Frank Mort, for example, claimed to detect a change between the 1950s and the 1980s among young men in the UK. He claimed that there had been an increase in individuality, articulated through the use of clothes, hair, body decoration and body movement, among young men. This had been *followed*, rather than simply *created*, by advertisers and marketing people. The advertisements, together with photographs attached to feature articles in the new men's magazines, contributed to a *sexualisation* of the male body in ways which had not been possible in the 1950s. This had spread to television advertisements by the early 1990s. The male imagery used is not as much macho as erotic, even narcissistic. Street culture is a matter of glances, looks, making a quick impression – it is a *visual* culture. (There is an echo here of the blasé attitude that Simmel noted in his

analysis of Berlin before 1910 discussed in Chapter 1.) Frank
Mort wrote about the newly emerging conceptions of masculinity
in the 1980s as follows:

> Imagine yourself on Tottenham High Road on a winter
> Saturday afternoon. The pavements are blocked, but not
> with Christmas shoppers. A continuous stream of male
> youths are making for the Spurs ground. Look once and
> it might be the rituals of class played out unchanged since
> the 50s. Look again. It *is* 1987, not 1957. What has
> changed are the surfaces of the lads themselves, the way
> they carry their masculinity. Individuality is on offer,
> incited through commodities and consumer display. From
> jeans: red tabs, designer labels, distressed denim. To
> hair: wedges, spiked with gel, or pretty hard boys who
> wear it long, set off with a large ear-ring.
>
> (Mort, 1988: 196)

To the casual observer, it might appear that little had changed
from earlier periods in the way in which young men were using
consumer items. One crucial change in the 1980s, which Mort
commented upon, was the change in what was desired. Mort
continued as follows:

> The rise and rise of advertising and marketing aimed at
> young men is part and parcel of the current enterprise
> boom in the service sector and media industries. But
> what is going on here is more subtle than advertising
> hype and the profit motive. Young men are being sold
> images which rupture traditional icons of masculinity.
> They are stimulated to look at themselves – and other
> men – as objects of consumer desire. They are getting
> pleasures previously branded taboo or feminine. A new
> bricollage of masculinity is the noise coming from the
> fashion house, the marketplace and the street.
>
> (Mort, 1988: 193–4)

Men have become as much a part of modern consumerism as
women. Their construction of a sense of who they are is
accomplished as much through style, clothing, body image and
the right look as is women's. This type of consumption is not so
much a trivial extra on top of 'real life' as a means of establishing
an identity. Consumption built around the human body – its
attractiveness to the self as much as to others; its sexual and

erotic appeal; its use as a means of expressing a sense of identity – has become a process in which desire is embedded, in which major meanings are located (Kellner, 1992).

One group of men have come to hold a particularly ambivalent place in western culture – male homosexuals. Homosexual men have been defined as pleasure-seeking consumers, hedonists, *par excellence*. Some, those in work particularly, continued to consume, for example, during the recession of the early 1990s, when others were struggling financially.

The taboo against male homosexuality had been successfully challenged during the 1960s and 1970s in western capitalist societies, with important, if unintended and unforeseen, consequences. Taboos define what is seen as polluting, unclean, dirty or forbidden in a culture (Douglas, 1970). The infringement of a taboo invokes, or provokes, disgust, anger and sometimes violent retribution. The development of a specifically gay sub-culture oriented towards gay men, and to a lesser extent to lesbian women, helped to break down the taboos which surround gay men and lesbian women. There developed a small, but nevertheless significant, gay sub-culture in many western metropolitan areas, based upon consumer patterns among gay men. These included the development of gay bars in which drinks were sold to men hoping to meet a partner, or who were just relaxing in a non-stigmatising environment (Blachford, 1981). There developed too more clothing stores for men; men in general were a growing market for clothing, and gay men often set up, or worked in, such shops. Newspapers, magazines and books related to gay issues developed; discos for gay men were started. Even particular holiday resorts developed for gays in Europe, north Africa, Asia and the United States, for instance.

These new commercial, gay businesses needed advertising in magazines and newspapers. Consequently, from the 1960s, a gay commercial world began to emerge in large cities and metropolitan areas in the western world. Most of these consumer patterns for gay men continued into the 1990s, providing a base for gay men within the heartland, as it were, of capitalist consumerism. This provided the gay community with some form of protection during the 1980s. Protection was needed because the arrival of AIDS had helped to reinforce the taboo against male homosexuality in the eyes of some politicians and some religious figures, for instance (Weeks, 1985: 44–53). The establishment of a gay consumer sub-culture had the unforeseen consequence, unforeseen that is by those who set up the early gay venues and businesses in the 1960s and 1970s, of providing some means of preserving a positive sense of identity for gay men during the moral panic about AIDS.

This moral panic reached its peak in the early to mid-1980s, when some of the western newspapers dubbed AIDS the 'gay plague'. This reaction had been especially strong in those cultures influenced by Anglo-Saxon puritanism. Anglican and Roman Catholic cultures were less condemnatory, even providing counselling and supportive care for those who were HIV positive, or had developed AIDS. However, at the level of official statements, the Vatican continued to reiterate its view in 1975 and in 1992 that homosexuality was sinful. (See, for example, a document from the Roman Catholic church produced by the Sacred Congregation for the Doctrine of the Faith, 1975: 10–11.) The Church of England was ambivalent, saying that gay relationships, which involved active sexual relations between two men, or two women, fell short of the ideal. Both churches defined homosexuality as being symptomatic of a materialistic, consumption-oriented culture, which they continued to see as being morally suspect, if not 'wrong'.

Gay men in other cultures, from Hindu Bombay to Saint Petersburg (formerly Leningrad) in Russia, began to assert their 'rights' to have places and spaces in which to meet, such as bars and discos, free from harassment by the police. This will lead, no doubt, to the development of a gay consumer culture in these non-western social formations too. It is one of the paradoxes of recent history that it seems to be the case that gay people are protected from being isolated and oppressed by developing a commercial, consumer-oriented, gay sub-culture. Some large companies have invested capital in discos, in popular music by gay groups, in public houses with a gay clientele, and in holidays aimed at gay people. As a consequence of this, many gay men do not share the criticism of the commercialisation of their patterns of consumption, a criticism voiced by some feminists and by social critics generally.

Between the 1970s and the 1990s, more men than previously in the twentieth century began to live alone, to leave wives and children, sometimes to live with another woman, who might herself have children from a previous marriage. More women actively and freely chose to live alone, or with other women, who might or might not have children. Between 1980 and 1990, for instance, the percentage of all births outside marriage increased from 11.8 per cent in 1980 to 28.3 per cent in 1990, and among those aged under 20 years the figure increased from 42.6 per cent in 1980 to 80.3 per cent in 1990 (HMSO, 1991). Some men desired to live alone, or with a woman, or with another man. An increasing number of younger women chose to live without a man around, or without being married.

There will be more men of all ages living without women in the 1990s than in the recent past. Men will continue to be targeted, no doubt, by advertisers and commercial groups as a distinct group of consumers, although there will be a variety of patterns of life-styles among the new male consumers.

Men – gays, bisexuals and 'straights' – are now as much a part of modern consumerism as women. Their construction of a sense of who they are, of their identity as men, is now achieved as much through style of dress and body care, image, the right 'look', as women's. This process of identity construction and maintenance among men need not necessarily displace a sense of identity derived from the world of work; in some cases it may be combined with such a source of identity. Nevertheless, there is an increasing number of men who now define themselves through their patterns of consumption rather than through a work-role identity. Work provides money for purchasing the consumer goods required to construct and maintain identity. For the unemployed, some may construct a sense of identity through the limited amount of consumption of music, clothing, eating and drinking patterns which they are able to afford, while others become unable to sustain an adequate sense of identity without a work role and without the money that provided a means for sustaining an identity through patterns of consumption.

Definitions of what constitutes a basic set of necessities for living have changed since 1950. The most important change is probably television – for over 96 per cent of the population of Britain have television, and just over two-thirds had access to a car in 1990. Refrigerators, electric cleaners and cookers, radios, telephones, cassette and/or record players, indoor toilets, bathrooms and central heating – all these have moved from being seen as 'luxury' items at the end of the Second World War to being perceived as 'necessities' in the last decade of the twentieth century (HMSO, 1991). Men who live alone, or who move from one household to another to live with another woman, or another man, experience the desire for these consumer goods; most regard them as essentials, as necessities, to living in the 1990s.

Consumption has become essential to many men's sense of who they are. It has become as significant as work roles, if not more so, for younger men especially. Consumption has entered into the unconscious sense of identity of men and women in the period since the 1950s. It has become a key aspect of recent forms of capitalism, and has enabled capitalism's symbols, and the products associated with them, to enter into the desires of the unconscious. The consumption of many goods is now linked with libidinal desires, sometimes in ways which were defined by the culture in the recent past as being perverse (Lyotard, 1974). But in this way consumption has made capitalism appear to be legitimate in a more profound way than in other periods of its development (Habermas, 1976). It promises the consummation and satisfaction of desires which still may not always speak their name.

In the 1970s and 1980s particularly, consumers were offered new sites for gazing at clothes, furniture, sports gear and foods and for buying – the shopping malls, or shopping centres, in which a large number of shops were found located under one roof, in one space. These shopping malls were built, typically, on out-of-town sites, at convenient points on new motorway networks near large centres of population. Typically they required a car for visiting them, although some were served by buses or trains. They often resulted in local shops closing down because local shopkeepers could not compete in volume terms, or price, with the new stores in the shopping malls – a problem for the old, the poor, those without cars in areas where local shops closed down. Some people could not easily find, or afford, transport to and from the shopping centres.

However, studies in Australia and the United States have shown that the unemployed, the old and the poor did visit shopping malls at least once a week. Their reasons for so doing were not necessarily for purchasing goods, but to stroll around, to see and be seen, to escape from climatic extremes outside to enter the cool, or the warmth, of the air-conditioned, controlled atmosphere of the shopping centres. One study in Australia, for example, found that '80 percent of unemployed young people visited the mall at least once a week, and nearly 100 percent of young unemployed women were regular visitors' (Fiske, 1989: 15). Fiske continued:

The youths consumed images and space instead of commodities, a kind of sensuous consumption that did not
create profits. The positive pleasure of parading up and
down, of offending 'real' consumers and the agents of
law and order, of asserting their difference within, and
different use of, the cathedral of consumerism became
an oppositional cultural practice.

(Fiske, 1989: 17)

There are echoes here of the *flâneurs* who Simmel and Baudelaire
noticed in the nineteenth century, although these earlier individuals were not necessarily protesting against bourgeois life *in
toto*. The late twentieth-century shopping 'mall walkers', as they
are called in Australia and the United States by the owners of
the malls in notices which welcome them, may or may not be
'oppositional' in their cultural practice, as Fiske suggests. It, no
doubt, depends on the form and content of the 'oppositional'
cultural practices. If these are mainly strolling around, not
buying, but also not stealing too much, and dressing in styles
which are not in the windows of the stores in the malls, 'mall
walkers' may be tolerated, even welcomed. If they involve
behaviour which 'real' customers complain about, or if the 'mall
walkers' indulge in theft on too large a scale for store managers
to tolerate, the welcome is likely to disappear. In its place appear
store detectives, mall detectives in plain clothes, police or uni-
formed guards, even dogs, and armed guards. In the United
States 'policing' of who is allowed entry to the malls has become
stricter in the last two or three decades of the twentieth century,
for both *bona fide* customers stop going to the malls and stores
managers complain if robbery, burglary or delinquent behaviour
is tolerated to too great an extent. The malls are there to make
profits, to sell goods and services, not to provide environments
for 'deviants' who refuse to spend, or who cannot afford to spend.
So although the shopping malls provide a space for the young,
the old and the poor that allows some groups to protest, to
counter the pressure to buy the consumer goods they cannot
afford, this protest is a protest on sufferance; it can be controlled
by the social control agencies of the owners and rent-payers of
the malls.

These spaces do not 'belong' to the counter-consumer culture
of protesting groups. Fiske over-estimated the degree to which
these groups can act as an effective agent of protest against

western capitalism's consumer culture and its goods. Many of the young male protesters, in any case, may change and join in consumerism as an ideology, and consumption as a practice, once they have married, have children and are buying their own homes – something which the vast majority do in Australia and the United States, and which over two-thirds of the population do in Britain. Any protest against a consumption-oriented life-style seems to be short-lived once young men and women are in paid employment; the unemployed aspire to it while unemployed and become consumers once in paid work roles. These forms of protest via consumption, which are discussed by Fiske, seem to be an easily absorbed form of protest in western capitalism; they are interesting side-lines rather than constituting a central attack on the ideology of consumerism or its associated practices.

Identities are constructed around the items purchased by varying groups of consumers, including distinctive groups of men. This proposition is one with some empirical bite, but it must be remembered that it belongs primarily to the fleshing out of an analytical model of the implications to be expected in postmodern forms of capitalism. The social and cultural construction of such identities has roots in people's unconscious desires too – the desires of homosexual men and women were treated here as being ideal-typical. Desires, both those socially, culturally learned from peer groups and the surrounding symbols in the wider culture, and those discovered to lie in, or to be thrusting up from, the unconscious, play a central role in the ways in which consumers in post-modern capitalism construct their social identities.

5

Conclusion

Consumption has become a process which typifies late modern, or 'post-modern', capitalism, as was discussed in Chapter 4. In so far as many people's sense of identity is now bound up with their patterns of consumption rather than their work roles, it can be said that a new phase of capitalism has emerged. This new phase may usefully be called 'post-modern' to distinguish it from earlier phases.

In the earlier phases of capitalism, work, that is work in paid employment roles, formed the core of many people's sense of identity, sometimes for women working outside the home as well as for men. Now, it is consumer goods and household patterns of consumption which play an important part in the social and cultural construction of identities for men, women and children. The question 'Who am I?' is one which is as likely to be answered in terms of consumption patterns as it is in terms of an occupational role by many people in western capitalism. For many young people, for instance, the question of who they think they are, or how they would like to live, is as likely to be answered in terms of the kind of consumer life-style they aim for as the kind of occupation they seek.

Some readers may be wondering in the back of their minds whether post-modern forms of consumption are a 'good thing' or a 'bad thing' – a straight-forward binary opposition à la Lévi-Strauss. The process of consumption cannot be appropriated into social thought, however, simply as a 'good thing' or as a 'bad thing'. It is both. Consumption has become one of the major processes in modern/post-modern capitalism which most affects the ordinary inhabitants of western countries. It is such ordinary people's hopes of being able to consume goods, and a growing variety of packaged consumer experiences from travel to sports, which has helped to legitimate capitalism since the 1950s. This is increasingly the case not only in the West, but among a growing number of groups of people in various social formations throughout the world.

The pleasures which are derived from the consumption of goods, and commercially packaged experiences, by ordinary people who can afford them are defined by most of those who buy them, and by many who cannot afford most of the items of modern consumption, as a 'good thing'. There are not many groups who are able to sustain a moral, or political, critique of consumption who can carry this critique into daily practice, for consumption is difficult, if not impossible, to avoid in capitalist social formations. It is difficult, for example, to 'deprive' children of consumer goods, such as the 'right' kind of clothing, or electronic games for their computers, if others in their peer group have such things, and the child's parent(s) can afford to purchase the desired items. Even during economic down-turns, recessions or depressions, consumption remains important as a hope, if not a practice, among people. The unemployed become depressed, if they do, not only because their sense of worth as workers is removed, but also because their role as providers for their families, providers of consumer items of all kinds, is lost.

Identities are changed, shattered or re-formed during such experiences. Not being able to consume, in the post-modern sense, becomes a source of deep discontent.

On the negative side of the dialectics of modern consumption, the environmental consequences of ever increasing numbers of people becoming able to consume an ever widening variety of consumer goods, to travel to ever more exotic, or formerly exotic, places, have become more severe at the end of the twentieth century than ever before. From the disposal of rubbish and old pieces of equipment, to the wearing down of the Pennine Way in England; from the over-crowding in the National Parks in the United States, to the over-crowded, dirty and polluted beaches around much of the Mediterranean; from pollution of the air from car exhaust fumes, or coal-fired electricity power generators, to the factory-farming methods used to produce the food supplies that consumers 'want', or will tolerate; modern/post-modern consumption is creating environmental problems which cannot be easily handled.

Yet consumer desires, once aroused, are difficult to control socially. For every convert to environmentalism in the West, there are probably at least two or three new consumers being produced and socialised somewhere in the world – perhaps many more. New technologies may well develop to help with the environmental problems which are a major consequence of ever spreading, ever increasing consumption, but they may not be enough, or in place in time, to prevent more catastrophes to the environment than have occurred already.

As more and more groups in the world become aware of the goods on offer by having their desires stimulated, formed and articulated by the mass media and modern advertising, so the number of people who form their sense of purpose and identity through 'consumption' expands. This process too has a positive aspect, as well as the negative aspect of adding to global environmental problems and to pollution. In so far as one of the main alternatives to the production of a sense of identity through consumption seems to lie in a sense of identity, and purpose, being derived from ethnic, racial or national group membership, frequently linked with acts of violence, mainly by men, to those who are defined as being 'different', consumerism might well be judged to be preferable.

The rise of nationalisms in some parts of the world, such as in what was formerly communist, Eastern Europe, Russia and the nations of the former Soviet Union, and in the Middle East, may be seen as a substitute, or an available alternative, to consumption, as a means of creating a sense of identity. This is particularly the case in social formations which have high rates of male unemployment. Ethnicity has been re-created, re-activated or reinvented by political and religious figures to form socio-cultural groups whose existence is marked out by establishing a sense of *difference* from others, from neighbouring groups. These processes have generated violence, wars, or mutual suspicions and intolerance towards other ethnic groups, in those parts of the world which have not entered fully into capitalism as a mode of production, let alone as a mode of consumption, in the last years of the twentieth century.

Weapons and ammunition arrive in some of these social formations, for instance, more easily than medicines, foods, colour televisions, cars, refrigerators or jeans. Consumption, by comparison, could be perceived as a preferable, peaceful, alternative to violent clashes in such parts of the world. In social formations where masculinity continues to be defined in terms of fighting, the arrival of a consumer culture, containing images of the 'new man' in which masculine identity is constructed around consumption patterns in clothing, cars, music or sports, might be seen as a form of social, even moral, progress by some, including many of the mothers and wives of the soldiers called up to do national service, to fight, in various societies which remain outside the core of post-modern capitalism.

The rise and rise of 'consumption' in the West, and now in more and more countries on the globe, raises problems, however, of how this process is to be theorised within social science. It is because consumption has entered the processes of identity formation and identity maintenance, that it has become so central to people's lives in western capitalism. It shows every sign of growing both in the West and elsewhere, rather than subsiding, in spite of periods of economic down-turn.

Jean Baudrillard, whose ideas were mentioned in Chapter 3, came close to connecting consumption with a social theory built initially upon the work of Marxism and Freudian psychoanalysis. Such a theory could have provided a useful basis for the social analysis of consumption, but Baudrillard seemed too eager to move beyond Marx and Freud. Baudrillard seems to have confused theoretical analysis with praxis, or practice. For instance, he wrote:

> Symbolic exchange is no longer an organising principle; it no longer functions at the level of modern social institutions. . . . And if a certain conception of the Revolution since Marx has tried cutting a path through [the] law of value, it has in the end remained a revolution according to the Law. As for psychoanalysis, although it acknowledges the ghostly presence of the symbolic, it averts its power by circumscribing it in the individual unconscious, reducing it, under the Law of the Father,

to the threat of Castration and the subversiveness of the Signifier. Always the Law.

(Baudrillard, 1988: 119)

In the cases of Marxism and psychoanalysis, Baudrillard took the practices, not the theory, as his point of criticism. It is the revolution, presumably that in Russia in 1917, that he has in mind in his critique of Marxism. But Marxism as a social theory and philosophy is about the next stage in the development of *advanced* forms of capitalism. It was not intended by Marx that it should be used as an ideology of legitimation by a party elite in a relatively economically backward social formation. Similarly, Baudrillard's criticism of psychoanalysis is directed towards the therapeutic practice of work with individuals, whereas Freud's own theory was highly social and cultural, and need not imply that therapy is to be used to construct conformists out of some types of non-conformist (Bocock, 1983: 60–7). These two theoretical approaches of Marxism and psychoanalysis seem still to have life left in them, and are difficult to surpass intellectually, despite numerous attempts to do so, of which Baudrillard's is one of the most recent and most daring.

Baudrillard argued that both Freudian and Marxist analyses of desires and of capitalism respectively had been overtaken by changes within capitalism. These changes concern 'the autonomy of the sign', or of what has been termed in this book the 'symbolic', following Langer's important distinction between sign and symbol, discussed in Chapter 3. Baudrillard's claim was that what he called signs (i.e. symbols in Langer's sense) no longer relate to 'the real', as they once seemed to do in earlier stages of capitalism's development, when Marx was writing, for instance. Then the concept of 'use-value' still could have meaning. Items could be interpreted as having clear uses, as in everyday actions such as eating or cleaning or keeping warm. Such uses could be established for most of what was then being produced and purchased.

In the late twentieth century, however, in post-modern capitalism, all this has changed, Baudrillard claims. What matters in this later form of commodity capitalism is the *disconnection* between the items purchased by consumers and 'the real'. The sign/symbolic has taken off into what Baudrillard called 'hyperreality', that is a realm of signs/symbols entirely unrelated to consumers' needs – they may happen to satisfy a 'need' but this has become accidental, as it were. The consumer goods of post-modernity are sold as symbols. They form their own kind of reality. Baudrillard wrote, for example: 'The entire strategy of the system lies in this hyper-reality of floating values' (Baudrillard, 1988: 122).

Concerning Freudian psychoanalysis, Baudrillard maintained that symbols, quintessentially dream symbols, had been seen as related to the desires of the human body, especially sexuality, and that this relation between symbols and the desires of the body had become severed in the late twentieth century. Once Freud could plausibly maintain that dream symbols could be interpreted by skilled and trained analysts; that dreams had a potentially decipherable meaning, albeit hidden in the unconscious. Now, in the late twentieth century, this is no longer the case. Signs/symbols float in hyper-reality, that is the contemporary socio-cultural system formed out of signs and symbols. Formerly unconscious desires are now articulated in the symbols of consumerism, in the advertisements and the packaging as much as in the goods themselves.

Post-modern capitalism thrives on the symbolic in the processes surrounding consumption. Even the desires of the young protesters of the late 1960s, who were opposed to the capitalist system, were absorbed into 'radical chic' clothing, music and the popular culture of the media. The symbols of protest generated profits for some; stylish products for consumers. Formerly forbidden desires, desires which are defined as being immoral in the eyes of some puritanical pressure groups, have been made the source of profits – as in the growth of consumer products for gay men since the 1960s.

Unconscious desires can never be fully satisfied, however, *pace* Baudrillard. The unconscious outwits the best laid plans of commerce, advertising and the modern/post-modern consumer industries. Consumerism promises to satisfy people's unconscious desires for pleasures, some of which were forbidden to earlier generations, such as the pleasures of the eroticised male body, which was discussed in Chapter 4. This is achieved by offering 'real' goods, or travel experiences, a 'real' sense of excitement. But these 'real' things cannot satisfy directly the unconscious desires that they promise to fulfil. The symbolic level intervenes.

What is desired in post-modern consumerism is not the 'real' chocolate, the 'real' car, or house and furniture, which is consumed. Rather these 'real' things are substitutes; the desires they purport to satisfy are symbolic desires, not biologically given needs unmediated by cultural symbolism. In this Baudrillard is correct. Yet the unconscious does not cease to operate, nor can it so easily be contained and neutralised by the purchasing of commercial goods. Rather, the unconscious works to outwit the best laid plans of the advertisers and the manufacturers in the commercial consumer-oriented industries. If consumption purports to satisfy sexual desires, by selling things which make the consumer more attractive, at whatever age, by promising to make the purchaser appear more desirable, more able to attain erotic satisfaction, other unconscious desires remain unsatisfied by consumption. Consumption offers the *promise* of satisfaction, not the 'real thing', which would be actual orgasmic satisfaction. In any case there are other desires which lurk in the unconscious – those of the death drive.

The death drives, or death instincts, seek destructive aggressive satisfactions, which are in part given release, directly or indirectly, by consumer sports such as soccer, boxing, fencing, hunting or whatever. The consumer-oriented forms of meditation, which arose during the 1960s, for instance, some of which involved the consumption of drugs, may also be analysed as linked with the satisfaction of the death instincts. The main aim of the death drive is the unconscious desire for the cessation of all external stimuli; 'Nirvana' as Freud called this state of near-death (Freud, 1920: 98). The states of stillness, or even of near-death experiences, achieved by the use of certain drugs, or meditation techniques, could be seen as drawing energy from what Freud called the unconscious death drive. Again, the symbolic level intervenes. No real satisfaction of these desires is obtained most of the time, but substitute gratification or titillation. Perhaps this is just as well! The popularity of television serials involving violent killing, among mainly younger audiences, may be seen as part of the way in which western cultures cater for the unconscious desires of Thanatos (Marcuse, 1969b: 90).

Consumption of the media, the arts and sports can be seen, therefore, as symbolic activity which is linked with unconscious desires of the death drives as well as of the sexual drives. Baudrillard, however, went on to invoke 'death' as the major, ultimate, weak point in capitalist consumerism. He argued, for example, that death was the only higher order code which had escaped incorporation into the code of consumerism. 'Perhaps only death . . . is of a higher order than the code. Only symbolic disorder can breach the code. Any system approaching perfect operationality is approaching its own death' (Baudrillard, 1988: 122).

This end of the system seems to have been a long time coming. It has been talked and written about since Marx's own work in the mid-nineteenth century. Capitalism is not only not dead yet, but spreading into the former communist countries of Europe.

Capitalism, it seems, is able to absorb the death drives too. It does so by absorbing them in some consumer experiences to provide substitute gratification for the death drives, as well as sexual impulses, at least to the satisfaction of some people in these social formations. This may well require that some people do become really hurt, killed or murdered, so that others can read about the events in newspapers or watch television programmes about such events. However, death has been absorbed into post-modern capitalist cultures, along with many forms of erstwhile deviant forms of sexuality. Children remain taboo as sex objects and as murder victims; but quite a number of readers appear willing to buy newspapers and books to read about these deviations. Cultural absorption is the name of this macabre game. Capitalism remains, stronger rather than weaker in the eyes of millions of people.

Consumerism has become the practical ideology of capitalism, one which legitimates capitalism in the daily lives and everyday practices of millions of inhabitants of western, and other, social formations. It taps into the unconscious desires of the affluent and the poor, both in the West and elsewhere. The desires of would-be consumers helped to destabilise the communist regimes of Eastern Europe. Consumer products, the advertisements for them, and the representations of them in numerous television programmes and movies, tap into unconscious desires and help to legitimate capitalism, not so much intellectually, or morally, but at the level of the unconscious. This has become increasingly a global phenomenon. Consumerism thus seems to be triumphant, but not entirely so.

The opposition to consumerism does not come now from communism. The former communist regimes' failure to deliver enough consumer goods produced popularly based changes in Europe and elsewhere. Dogmatic Marxism, the ideology of communist regimes, should be distinguished, however, from Marxism as a social philosophical theory of alienation in capitalism. If this is done, as outlined in Chapter 2, consumption appears as one of the main ways by which alienation continues, even deepens, by entering into the psychic lives of people in advanced forms of capitalism. It does this by tapping into the level of unconscious desires.

Marx's theory of alienation, rather than the economistic versions of 'scientific' Marxism, can provide a way of grounding the analysis of consumption in a more philosophical manner as discussed in Chapter 2. Something like this is needed in order to overcome the alienated, and alienating, forms of consumption, at first at the philosophical level. The philosophical critique can later become translated into a praxis – a form of activity which links theory to practical social actions. This is necessary in the eyes of some – the ecologists and green-minded scientists and technologists, for instance – before post-modern forms of consumption destroy the ecological balance of the planet earth. There may be between fifty and one hundred years left before something cracks: the ozone layer becomes irreparably damaged, or global climate changes produce rising sea levels which flood many of the major inhabited areas of the world, for example.

There remains little to be found as a basis for critique and action in the modernist technological project, for this has played a large part in producing the problems of too much cónsumption without regard to the environmental consequences in both capitalism and in still existing, as well as in the former, communist regimes. Will there be a change of attitudes, so that people alter their desires as much as possible away from consumer goods and experiences into other dimensions of activity and experience? One powerful cultural and social-psychological institution which could do this in various parts of the world is religion.

The world's religions have provided satisfaction for the desires of the unconscious in earlier epochs, sometimes with psychologically damaging consequences, but at other times with more positive outcomes. There are indications that they can continue to provide such unconscious satisfaction, even in technologically advanced social formations. There are signs that religion has grown in the United States, for instance, since the 1940s, but it has not developed in such a way yet that it provides social and moral controls upon excessive material consumption. The United States is both more 'religious' than Britain or other parts of Western Europe, and is the inheritor of a puritanical discourse which was critical of too much material consumption, of excess. This critical discourse may well be revitalised, in conjunction with environmentalists and ecologists, in the future, to produce a new, broadly based social movement which could begin to criticise and to contain post-modern consumerism in practice.

The non-western countries in the world, where traditional religions appear to be still in place, religions such as Hinduism, Judaism, Islam, Christianity, Buddhism, even forms of Confucianism, continue to be affected by an increase in the desire for consumption. Consumption in many of these social formations involves material requirements, such as food, clean water, shelter, medical supplies and transport systems, but it is not restricted to these basic items. It seems that as soon as the basics are in place, and can be largely taken for granted as part of a daily routine, and excepting periodic crises in supplies of such basic items, the desires for the less essential items of modern/post-modern living, such as transistor radios, audio-cassettes, jeans, even cars and televisions, begin to emerge. The young in many regions outside of the western capitalist social formations are tuned into the consumer culture on an ever increasing scale.

Religious critiques of the ideology of consumerism, in advanced capitalist social formations, as well as in other social formations, may be more important for the future of the planet earth than has been realised so far. Is there likely to be a new puritanism? Is there, indeed, a requirement for such a religiously grounded moral system to constrain the global growth of consumption of more and more goods and experiences? If there is such a requirement from the point of view of environmentalism, will it not have to draw upon already existing discourses such as those which may be found in the world religions? It seems to be more intelligent for educated people, who see the environmental problems that modern/post-modern consumption can cause, to work with the nature-conserving components of the world religions, rather than to ignore, or even attack, religious discourses. Religions are more likely to be authoritarian, and to be negative in their social and cultural effects, if the more educated withdraw from them, or ignore them. If, on the other hand, the more educated engage with religious institutions, the world's religions are more likely to become effective agents of change, critical both of the damaging effects of consumption and of the authoritarianism in religions as well as in politics (Aquinas, 1959).

Religious discourses could, indeed still do, provide many people throughout the world with grounded reasons and motivational patterns for limiting their desires for consumer goods and experiences. Religious figures face great difficulties, however, in counteracting the messages of the mass media and advertising media for more and more consumption, but these difficulties may not be insurmountable for all time. Religious discourses may well be an important resource, allied with environmentalism, in developing a different attitude towards the world of nature. Nature, in the form of plants and animals, rivers and forests, is frequently seen as something to be cared for rather than ruthlessly exploited in the great world religions. (See Weber, 1970: Chapter XIII.)

This value-orientation could provide a useful starting point for a religiously based discourse, critical of consumerism as the main ideology of the future. The epoch of the exploitation of nature by consumption-oriented capitalism, and by materialistic forms of communism, is coming to an end – or rather it probably must come to an end if the earth is to continue to support human beings in a sustainable way of life. The world religions are an important resource of moral values, of caring orientations towards nature, and for providing a critique of capitalist consumption patterns if they can be disengaged from ethnic groups' rivalries for territory. The world's religions remain in contact with millions of ordinary people in the world, unlike the atheistic positivism derived from the Enlightenment of some western intellectuals and some materialistic communists. The world religions could help in overcoming the ideology of consumerism, and the social-economic practices associated with consumption, before the damage to the planet is too great to sustain 'civilised' forms of living.

Bibliography

Allen, J. (1992) 'Fordism and modern industry', Chapter 5 in Allen, J., Braham, P. and Lewis, P. (eds) *Political and Economic Forms of Modernity*, Cambridge: Polity Press.

Althusser, L. (1969) *For Marx*, London: Allen Lane.

Aquinas, T. (1959) *Selected Political Writings*, translated by Dawson, J., edited by D'Entreves, A.P., Oxford: Basil Blackwell.

Aristotle (1966) *Ethics* (The Nicomachean Ethics), Harmondsworth: Penguin Books

Ayer, A.J. (1946) *Language, Truth and Logic*, London: Gollancz.

Barthes, R. (1972) *Mythologies*, London: Jonathan Cape Ltd.

Baudrillard, J. (1988) *Selected Writings*, Cambridge: Polity Press.

Bauman, Z. (1992) *Intimations of Postmodernity*, London: Routledge.

Blachford, G. (1981) 'Male dominance and the gay world', Chapter 8 in Plummer, K. (ed.) *The Making of the Modern Homosexual*, London: Hutchinson.

Bocock, R. (1976) *Freud and Modern Society,* London: Routledge.

Bocock, R. (1983) *Sigmund Freud*, London: Routledge.

Bocock, R. (1986) *Hegemony*, London: Routledge.

Bocock, R. and Thompson, K. (eds) (1992) *Social and Cultural Forms of Modernity*, Cambridge and Oxford: Blackwell and Polity Press.

Bottomore, T. and Rubel, M. (1971) *Karl Marx. Selected Writings in Sociology and Social Philosophy,* Harmondsworth: Penguin Books.

Bourdieu, P. (1984) *Distinction: A Social Critique of the Judgement of Taste*, translated by Nice, R., Cambridge: Harvard University Press.

Bourdieu, P. (1989) 'Social space and symbolic power', in *Sociological Theory,* Volume 7: 14–25.

Bowlby, R. (1987) 'Modes of shopping: Mallarmé at the Bon Marché', in Armstrong, N. and Tennenhouse, L. (eds) *The Ideology of Conduct*, pp.185–205, New York: Methuen.

Callinicos, A. (1991) *The Revenge of History: Marxism and East European Revolutions*, Cambridge: Polity Press.

Campbell, C. (1987) *The Romantic Ethic and the Spirit of Modern Consumerism*, Oxford: Basil Blackwell.

Cashmore, E. (1979) *Rastaman,* London: Allen and Unwin.

Cohen, S. (1973) *Folk Devils and Moral Panics*, London: Paladin.

Cowling, M. and Wilde, L. (eds) (1989) *Approaches to Marx,* Milton Keynes and Philadelphia: Open University Press.

Dallmayr, F. (1991) *Life-world, Modernity and Critique: Paths between Heidegger and the Frankfurt School*, Cambridge and Oxford: Polity Press.

Deleuze, G. and Guattari, F. (1977) *Anti-Oedipus. Capitalism and Schizophrenia,* New York: Viking Press.

Dosse, F. (1991) *Histoire du Structuralisme. I. Le champ du signe, 1945–66*, Paris: Editions La Découverte.

Douglas, M. (1966) *Purity and Danger. An Analysis of Concepts of Pollution and Danger*, Harmondsworth: Penguin Books.

Douglas, M. (1970) *Natural Symbols. Explorations in Cosmology*, London: Barrie & Rockcliffe: The Cresset Press.

Dunning, E., Murphy, P. and Williams, J. (1988) *The Roots of Football Hooliganism,* London: Routledge.

Durkheim, E. (1961) *The Elementary Forms of the Religious Life,* New York: Collier Books.

Elias, N. (1978) *The Civilizing Process, Volume 1: The History of Manners*, Oxford: Basil Blackwell.

Erikson, E. (1950) *Childhood and Society*, New York: W.W.

Norton Inc. Revised edition (1965) Penguin Books: Harmondsworth.

Erikson, E. (1968) *Identity: Youth and Crisis,* London: Faber & Faber.

Featherstone, M. (1990) *Consumer Culture and Post-modernism,* London: Sage.

Featherstone, M. (1991) 'The body in consumer culture', in Featherstone, M., Hepworth, M. and Turner, B. (eds) *The Body. Social Process and Cultural Theory,* London: Sage.

Featherstone, M. (1992) 'Post-modernism and the aestheticization of everyday life', in Lash, S. and Friedman, J. (eds) *Modernity and Identity,* Oxford: Basil Blackwell.

Fiske, J. (1989) *Reading the Popular,* Boston, USA: Unwin Hyman, Inc.

Frank, A.W. (1991) 'For a sociology of the body: an analytical review', in Featherstone, M., Hepworth, M. and Turner, B. (eds) *The Body. Social Process and Cultural Theory,* London: Sage.

Freud, S. (1900) *The Interpretation of Dreams,* available in the Pelican Freud Library (1976 edition), Harmondsworth.

Freud, S. (1904) *The Psychopathology of Everyday Life,* Berlin: Krager and Harmondsworth: Pelican Freud Library.

Freud, S. (1905) *Three Essays on the Theory of Sexuality,* Harmondsworth: Pelican Freud Library.

Freud, S. (1916 and 1974) *Introductory Lectures on Psychoanalysis,* Volume 1, Harmondsworth: Penguin Books.

Freud, S. (1920) *Beyond the Pleasure Principle,* Harmondsworth: Pelican Freud Library.

Friedman, J. (1992) 'Narcissism, roots and post-modernity: the constitution of selfhood in the global crisis', in Lash, S. and Friedman, J. (eds) *Modernity and Identity,* Oxford: Basil Blackwell.

Frisby, D. (1984) *Georg Simmel,* London: Routledge.

Fukuyama, F. (1989) 'The end of history?', *The National Interest,* No. 16. USA.

Galbraith, J. (1963) *Affluent Society,* Harmondsworth: Penguin Books.

Gamble, A. (1981) *Britain in Decline,* London: Macmillan.

Gerth, H. and Wright Mills, C. (eds) (1970) *From Max Weber,* London: Routledge.

Giddens, A. (1971) *Capitalism and Modern Social Theory,* Cambridge: Cambridge University Press.

Giddens, A. (1991) *Modernity and Self-identity: Self and Society in the Late Modern age*, Cambridge: Polity Press.

Goldthorpe, J. *et al*. (1968–9) *The Affluent Worker in the Class Structure*, 3 vols., Cambridge: Cambridge University Press.

Gramsci, A. (1971) edited by Hoare, Q. and Nowell Smith, G. *Selections from the Prison Notebooks of Antonio Gramsci*, London: Lawrence & Wishart.

Habermas, J. (1976) *Legitimation Crisis,* London: Heinemann.

Habermas, J. (1984) *Theory of Communicative Action*, Vol. 1. Cambridge: Polity Press.

Hall, S. (1988) 'Thatcher's lessons', in *Marxism Today*, March 1988: 20–7.

Hall, S. (1992) 'Our mongrel selves', in *New Statesman & Society*, 19 June, London.

Hamilton, P. (1983) *Talcott Parsons*, London: Routledge.

Harland, R. (1987) *Superstructuralism. The Philosophy of Structuralism and Post-Structuralism*, London: Methuen.

Harvey, D. (1989) *The Condition of Post-modernity*, *An Enquiry into the Origins of Cultural Change*, Oxford: Basil Blackwell.

HMSO (1991) *Population Trends*, Vol. 65.

Jacoby, R. (1975) *Social Amnesia,* Hassocks, Sussex: Harvester Press; USA: Beacon Press.

Jameson, F. (1983) 'Post-modernism and consumer society', in Foster, H. (ed.) *Post-modern Culture,* London: Pluto Press.

Jessop, B. (1989) 'Conservative regimes and the transition to post-Fordism', in Gottdiener, M. and Komminos, N. (eds) (1989), *Capitalist Development and Crisis Theory*, London and Basingstoke, Macmillan.

Kellner, D. (1992) 'Popular culture and the construction of post-modern identities', in Lash, S. and Friedman, J. (eds) *Modernity and Identity*, Oxford: Basil Blackwell.

Kristeva, J. (1980) *Desire in Language. A Semiotic Approach to Literature and Art*, Oxford: Basil Blackwell.

Lacan, J. (1977) *Ecrits. A Selection*, London: Tavistock Publications.

Lacan, J. (1979) *The Four Fundamental Concepts of Psychoanalysis*, translated by Sheridan, A., Harmondsworth: Penguin Books.

Langer, S. (1951) *Philosophy in a New Key, A Study in the Symbolism of Reason, Rite, and Art*, Cambridge, USA: Harvard University and Mentor Books.

Lash, S. and Friedman, F. (eds) (1992) *Modernity and Identity,* Oxford: Basil Blackwell.

Leach, E. (1969) *Genesis as Myth and Other Essays*, London: Jonathan Cape.

Leonard, C. (1991) 'One for the boys', in *The Times: City Diary*, London: Times Newspapers.

Lévi-Strauss, C. (1966) *The Savage Mind (La Pensée Sauvage)*, London: Weidenfeld & Nicolson.

Lévi-Strauss, C. (1969) *Totemism,* Harmondsworth: Pelican Books.

Lyotard, J.-F. (1974) *Economie Libidinale,* Paris: Les Editions de Minuit.

Lyotard, J. F. (1984) *The Postmodern Condition*, Manchester: Manchester University Press.

MacIntyre, A. (1988) *Whose Justice? Which Rationality?,* London: Duckworth.

Marcuse, H. (1969a) *An Essay on Liberation*, London: Allen Lane, The Penguin Press.

Marcuse, H. (1969b) *Eros and Civilization*, London: Sphere Books.

Marx, K. (1959) *Economic and Philosophic Manuscripts of 1844*, London: Lawrence & Wishart.

Marx, K. and Engels, F. (1974) *The German Ideology,* London: Lawrence & Wishart.

Mead, M. (1962) *Male and Female*, Harmondsworth: Penguin Books.

Meszaros, I. (1970) *Marx's Theory of Alienation*, London: Merlin Press.

Miller, D. (1987) *Material Culture and Mass Consumption*, Oxford: Basil Blackwell.

Mitchell, J. (1971) *Woman's Estate*, Harmondsworth: Penguin Books.

Mitchell, J. (1974) *Psychoanalysis and Feminism,* Harmondsworth: Penguin Books.

Mort, F. (1988) 'Boy's own? Masculinity, style and popular culture', in Chapman, R. and Rutherford, J. (eds) *Male Order*, London: Lawrence & Wishart.

O'Brien, S. and Ford, R. (1988) 'Can we at last say goodbye to social class?', *Journal of the Market Research Society*, Vol. 30, No. 3, pp. 289–332.

Pivcevic, E. (1970) *Husserl and Phenomenology*, London: Hutchinson.

Plummer, K. (ed.) (1981) *The Making of the Modern Homosexual,* London: Hutchinson.

Porter, R. (1990) *English Society in the Eighteenth Century,* 2nd edition, Harmondsworth, Penguin.

Sacred Congregation for the Doctrine of the Faith (1975) *Declaration on Certain Questions Concerning Sexual Ethics,* London: Catholic Truth Society.

Simmel, G. (1903) 'The metropolis and mental life', reprinted in Levine, D. (1971) *On Individuality and Social Form,* Chicago: University of Chicago Press.

Smart, B. (1993) *Postmodernity,* London: Routledge.

Thompson, E.P. (1963) *The Making of the English Working Class,* Harmondsworth: Penguin Books.

Tiger, L. (1969) *Men in Groups,* London: Nelson.

Timpanaro, S. (1976) *The Freudian Slip,* London: New Left Books.

Tomlinson, A. (1990) *Consumption, Identity and Style: Marketing Meanings and the Packaging of Pleasure,* London: Routledge.

Varma, V. (1993) *How and Why Children Hate: A Study of Conscious and Unconscious Sources,* London: Jessica Kingsley Ltd.

Veblen, T. (1912 and 1953) *The Theory of the Leisure Class: An Economic Study of Institutions,* New York: Mentor Books.

Wallis, R. and Bruce, S. (1986) *Sociological Theory, Religion and Collective Action,* Part IV, Belfast: Queen's University.

Weber, M. (1904 and 1949) *The Methodology of the Social Sciences,* translated by Shils, E. and Finch, H., Glencoe, Illinois: The Free Press.

Weber, M. (1915 and 1970) 'The social psychology of the world religions', in Gerth, H. and Wright Mills, C. (eds) (1970) *From Max Weber,* London: Routledge.

Weber, M. (1971) *The Protestant Ethic and the Spirit of Capitalism,* translated by Parsons, T., London: G. Allen & Unwin.

Weeks, J. (1977) *Coming Out. Homosexual Politics in Britain from the Nineteenth Century to the Present,* London: Quartet Books.

Weeks, J. (1985) *Sexuality and its Discontents. Meanings, Myths and Modern Sexualities,* London: Routledge.

Weeks, J. (1992) 'The body and sexuality', in Bocock, R. and Thompson, K. (eds) *Social and Cultural Forms of Modernity,* Cambridge and Oxford: Blackwell and Polity Press.

Weiss, F. G. (ed.) (1974) *Hegel: The Essential Writings,* New York and London: Harper & Row.

Wilde, L. (1989) 'The early development of Marx's concept of contradiction', Chapter 2 in Cowling, M. and Wilde, L. (eds) *Approaches to Marx*, Milton Keynes and Philadelphia: Open University Press.

Williams, R. (1958) *Culture and Society*, London: Chatto & Windus.

Williamson, J. (1986) *Consuming Passions: The Dynamics of Popular Culture*, London: Marian Boyars.

Willis, P. (1990) *Common Culture*, Milton Keynes: Open University Press.

Wittgenstein, L. (1958) *Philosophical Investigations*, translated by Anscombe, G., Oxford: Basil Blackwell.

Author index

Subject index